THIS PLACE IN ALL ITS SEASONS
THE HENRY FONDA HOME IN NEBRASKA

RUTH McCAULEY

Copyright 2000 by Ruth McCauley. All rights reserved. No part of this publication may be reproduced, stored in a retrieval system, or transmitted in any form or by any means, electronic, mechanical, photocopied, recorded, or otherwise, without the prior written permission of the publisher.

ISBN 1-886225-46-X
Library of Congress Catalog Number: 99-69875
Cover design by Angie Johnson Art Productions

Dageforde Publishing, Inc.
122 South 29th Street
Lincoln, Nebraska 68510
Phone: (402) 475-1123 Fax: (402) 475-1176
email: info@dageforde.com

Visit our web site at
www.dageforde.com

Printer in the United States of America
10   9   8   7   6   5   4   3   2   1

Dedicated to

> William Brace Fonda
> Herberta Jaynes fonda
> Mrs. Peter "Becky" Fonda
> My Dearest Bob

Contents

FOREWORD vii
PREFACE ix
ACKNOWLEDGMENTS xi
THE BEGINNING...AND THE END 1
OUR HENRY FONDA 4
THE HOUSE 9
THE HENRY FONDA I KNOW 13
THE WILLIAM BRACE FONDAS TRAVEL WEST 19
HALEY'S COMET 23
THE FONDAS IN GRAND ISLAND 25
WHAT MIGHT HAVE BEEN...AND WHAT WAS 29
AT THE OMAHA COMMUNITY PLAYHOUSE 31
NEW YORK AND CAPE COD 34
LETTER TO DAD 35
ELIZA SONNELAND CLARK WALKS WITH HENRY FONDA . 37
OMAHA PLAYHOUSE HONORS HENRY FONDA 39
A VISIT WITH EVA MARIE SAINT 42
CATCHING UP WITH DAVID RINTELS 44
STORIES OF FONDA 46
A BIRTHDAY CELEBRATION 51
HALLMARK CHRISTMAS CARD 54
CHRISTMAS AT THE FONDA COTTAGE, 1995 56
A CHRISTMAS STORY COMES FULL CIRCLE 62

PETER FONDA REMEMBERS CHRISTMASES	63
THE VISIT	64
PLANNING HENRY FONDA DAY	68
HENRY FONDA DAY	72
PETER FONDA'S WORKSHOP	74
LUNCHEON	76
HENRY FONDA MEMORIAL HIGHWAY	77
A VISIT TO THE BIRTHPLACE	79
DINNER	82
MAY 16, 1905	85
FLYING KITES WITH HENRY	92
SUNDAY BREAKFAST	95
BESSIE'S SUGAR COOKIES	98
THE HENRY FONDA ROSE GARDEN	101
HAPPY BIRTHDAY HENRY FONDA	106
THE HENRY FONDA ROSE	109
DEEP ROOTS DO FONDAS GROW	110
"I LOVE OMAHA"	112
GREAT PLAINS FILM FESTIVAL	114
BREAKFAST—TUPELO HONEY	117
MY FRIEND BECKY	118
SUE FONDA REMEMBERS	120
THE TURNER SANDHILLS RANCH	125
FRIENDS OF HENRY FONDA	126
AFTERWARD	129
ABOUT THE AUTHOR	135

FOREWORD

I was there in the Christmas of 1984 when Ruth McCauley began her journey to discover Henry Fonda's legacy to the Heartland. She and her husband, Bob, had decorated the Fonda birthplace in Grand Island, Nebraska, for Christmas and had come to share the story with readers of the *Omaha World-Herald*. Few writers have been as relentless in their search for detail or as dedicated in their pursuit of truth. Ruth has instilled in her biographic memoir an understanding of her subject that transcends the facts she has uncovered. She has traversed the heart of Henry Fonda with the sensitivity as only a fellow Nebraskan could do. Ruth often commented how grateful she would have been to have met her subject face to face. Indeed, readers of Ruth's sentimental journey will conclude that Mr. Fonda would have shared the gratitude.

Chris Olson
A Friend & Editor

The Fonda cottage in summer

PREFACE

This book has been written about a personal and pleasant relationship afforded me by a famous Hollywood family. I feel it lends information not written before about the life of the late Henry Fonda, and about his family today and what they have given to the Heartland of America.

It is about the house where it all started, and where anything after would always have its beginnings.

It contains stories from friends and family. In his book, *Don't Tell Dad*, Peter Fonda wrote how he told Jane that it seemed proper to dispose of Henry's ashes over the Platte River near Grand Island, where Henry was born. According to Henry's will, he was to be thrown out with the trash after he was cremated.

Disposing of Henry's ashes in the Platte River would certainly make sense because, after leaving Grand Island, the Platte River eventually flows into the Missouri River, just outside Henry's beloved Omaha— west of New York and east of Hollywood.

And there are my own stories. Fonda was known for the bees he kept and the jars of honey he collected that he would give to his theatrical colleagues, plus he always had a jar ready for the knowing hostess who invited him and Shirlee to dinner. How could I ever know that I would receive one of those coveted jars of honey? Not in my wildest dreams. But now, sitting on a shelf in my cupboard, is a jar given to me by Peter and Becky from the supply Henry gave them.

It all comes down to a reply Henry gave when he said, "Part of the secret of good life is having good friends."

ACKNOWLEDGMENTS

First, thanks to my editor, Chris Olson, who has encouraged me in this project and who wrote the first article for the *Omaha World-Herald* about the Fonda Christmas Tree in 1984. Our professional relationship has been a source of many ideas that brought this book full circle to completion.

Thanks to the Stuhr Museum of the Prairie Pioneer that has let me work in the place most dear to my heart—the Fonda cottage.

To Peter and Becky Fonda, without whom this book could not have happened.

And there are more...

My niece, Lori Jenson; Sandi Yoder, ex-director of the Stuhr Museum; the Omaha Community Playhouse; the *Grand Island Independent*; the *Omaha World-Herald*; the *Lincoln Journal Star*; Ken Bolton; the Friends of Henry Fonda and newsletter; Sources Unlimited in Fonda, N.Y.; Tom Anderson of the Prairie Pioneer Press, St. Stephen's Episcopal Church; the little girl at the Harry Truman birthplace; Harriet Fonda Warren; Douw and Sue Fonda; Shirlee Fonda; Jane Fonda; Ted Turner; Mary Shanley; Warren Rodgers;

THIS PLACE IN ALL ITS SEASONS

David Rintels; Eva Marie Saint; Jackson Perkins; Nancy Butler; the late Jack Learned; Lew Cole; Dr. Robert Manley; Jessie Walker; Paul Slimak of *Victorian Homes and Lifestyles*; Liza Sonneland Clark; Hallmark Cards Archives; the film industry; Janelle Lindberg; the Omaha Press Club; Cape Playhouse; Forest Lawn Cemetery; and the Great Plains Film Festival.

I must mention artist Angie Johnson who created the cover for this book and editor Sheila Reiter who spent time with me at the house and helped with the final manuscript.

And for these books:
Fonda My Life as told to Howard Teichmann
Henry Fonda—A Biography by Allen Roberts and Max Goldstein
The Fondas—A Hollywood Dynasty by Peter Collier
Don't Tell Dad by Peter Fonda
The Fondas by John Springer
Henry Fonda—A Celebration of the Life and Work of One of America's Beloved Actors by Norm Goldstein & Associated Press

For Earl

THE BEGINNING...AND THE END

> *We shall not cease from exploration*
> *And the end of all our exploring*
> *Will be to arrive where we started*
> *And know the place for the first time.*
> —T.S. Elliot

*I*t is springtime in Nebraska. The day is May 16th, the birthday of Henry Jaynes Fonda.
 I am having early morning coffee at the old round oak table in the dining room across from the bedroom where Henry Fonda was born. I feel such serenity listening to the song of the meadowlark outside on a fence post through the open front door of this little green cottage with the house number 622. The bay windows look upon a country setting. The breeze from the northwest and the aroma of coffee mix with the scent of the yellow roses blooming in the Henry Fonda Rose Garden in the arboretum a few yards away. Across the road is the field where we fly kites for Henry on his birthday because he and his father, W.B. Fonda, liked to fly kites on Sunday.

THIS PLACE IN ALL ITS SEASONS

Thoughts come easily in this cottage. Silent and quieting, this is a special place. I am thinking of the book I am writing and how it all came about. This day, this time, and this house make it easy. It is all planted here. I feel passionately drawn to this house like a relative from the past who, just one more time, wants to visit. I don't have any idea if any of the long-ago branch of my Whitney-Fonda relatives ever visited here since this home of Henry Fonda became a national shrine of sorts on these Stuhr Museum grounds on this Nebraska prairie.

I know every inch of this house by heart. I have decorated it. The painted grained soft wood floor, the authentic patterned wallpapers of the late 1800s, especially the paper in the bathroom with its pulverized glass embedded into the pattern. While most of the furniture is light oak, the phonograph and piano are made of mahogany, and the bedroom dresser is birds-eye maple. The woodwork is hardwood that has been painted, grained, and varnished. Wooden beads hang from the double doorway between the dining room and the parlor with the unusual 1855 Westminster parlor stove and its Isinglass panels and tiles that we decorate at Christmas. The staff writer Paul Slimak from the New York-based publication *Victorian Decorating and Lifestyles* wrote that the house has an "atmosphere of soft-spoken integrity and old-fashioned decency, very much like the roles Henry played in his screen career. Indeed, his presence here is palpable."

While I go back into the kitchen to refill my coffee cup from the pot on the old black South Bend wood stove, my thoughts turn to Christmases I have spent here and how the Friends of Henry Fonda group magically transforms this humble little cottage into a Christmas spectacular. To me, this kitchen is the heart of the home, the hearth where Herberta must have spent many happy hours with her baby

THE BEGINNING...AND THE END

son while cooking supper or baking her Thin Cookies from a recipe I now have.

On my way back to the table, I pass the nursery. There is a little white crib, the commode, the neatly folded diapers, baby booties, a tray with baby hair brush and comb, a patchwork quilt, diaper bag, and rocking chair. Also, there is the wicker baby buggy taken outside the house for the Fonda family reunion in 1992 that everyone used as a prop for photos.

Going back to the dining room, I pass through the bedroom with its brass bed. In the mirror of the dresser, I catch a glimpse of an old wind-up alarm clock on the bedside stand that might have been like the one that told the time of Henry's birth as recorded on his birth certificate.

Back in the kitchen, on the south wall, is a telephone like the one that they may have used on May 16, 1905, to call Dr. Roeder that a baby was on the way.

The curtains are stirring. In an antique glass basket, the beautiful tulips, lilacs, and other spring flowers for Henry's birthday celebration have arrived by carrier from the Fondas and been placed in the center of the dining room table. I hear guests coming up the brick walk. It is now 11 A.M., and it's time to light the candles and cut and serve the birthday cake.

OUR HENRY FONDA
The Boy from Grand Island

Although he grew to manhood in Omaha, Henry Fonda was born in Grand Island, Nebraska, on May 16, 1905, the son of William Brace Fonda and Herberta Jaynes Fonda. The event rated a news item in the *Grand Island Independent* on May 17, 1905. Fonda's father had been a commercial printer in both Grand Island and Omaha, but the report at the time of his son's birth suggested that he was selling a popular brand of crackers.

The Fondas were descended from a titled Italian who fled Genoa for the Netherlands several centuries earlier to escape political persecution. In 1642, the first Fondas came to America and settled in upper New York state to farm. The Fonda descendants founded the town of Fonda, New York, and later became western pioneers.

Henry's grandfather, Ten Eyck, came west after the Civil War to Omaha where Henry's father was born. William and Herberta Fonda had lived in Grand Island about a year and a half before Henry was born. Little did Dr. Roeder know he was delivering a baby who would grow up to become one of America's most gifted, famous, and beloved stage and screen actors of all time. Henry Fonda's theatrical career spanned five decades.

So it was, in this little cottage, Henry Fonda made his debut, uttered his first cry, and earned his first press notice in the morning paper. A glance at the family album shows Henry as a well-fed baby dressed in finely laundered clothes—a clear indication of his mother's concern over the child's welfare. Henry spoke of his mother as "an angelic woman." She was very attractive and musical, as well. Herberta Fonda liked to sing and play the piano while her husband accompanied her on the guitar.

The Fondas spent their first Christmas with their baby son in Grand Island. Uncle Ten Eyck Fonda, Jr. and Aunt Ethelyn came by train from Omaha for the holiday and to witness Henry's christening the following day, December 26, 1905, at St. Stephen's Episcopal Church.

Henry's parents, Herberta and William, outside their home in Grand Island, Nebraska, October, 1904. Herberta is pregnant with Henry at this time. (Stuhr archives)

Studio photograph of Henry Jaynes Fonda, 1905.
(Harriet Fonda Warren)

OUR HENRY FONDA

Henry in buggy at the age of 4 months.
(Stuhr Archives)

THIS PLACE IN ALL ITS SEASONS

Jane Fonda, her son Troy, and her cousin, Susan Casper, at Fonda Cemetery in Fonda, New York. (Montgomery County Department of History & Archives, Fonda, New York)

THE HOUSE

Henry Fonda's birthplace was built in 1884 on the 600 block of West Division Street as the home of William H. Hooper. In 1890, George B. Bell acquired the house. It was Bell who rented the home to the Fonda family in 1904. Although the Catholic Diocese in Grand Island donated the house to the Stuhr Museum, it was Fonda who provided the funds to move the structure to the museum grounds in August 1966. The Grand Island Diocese had obtained the land for the erection of a new convent. At that time, the house had been scheduled for demolition. Fonda, while acting on Broadway, learned of the situation from Grand Island acquaintance Dan Searle, then president of radio station KMMJ, and pledged his support to save the house.

While returning to the West Coast from New York, Fonda stopped in Grand Island in July, 1966 to make the final arrangements with Stuhr Museum officials for the preservation of the house. Fonda liked Stuhr Museum's concept and supported the museum's development until his death. That the internationally known architect Edward Durell Stone had designed the museum building was enough for him. On his last visit to his birthplace in 1978, Fonda stood in the bedroom where he was born. According to museum official Lew Cole, Fonda "quietly walked through each of the rooms, studying details of the furniture, walls, and floors. He stood looking at the brass bed for several minutes with a distant gaze. Then, he said, 'That's enough,' and walked out the door."

When Henry Fonda died in 1982, Stuhr Museum lost a true friend.

Starting with his birth, this bustling railroad town of Grand Island, Nebraska, would be the home of the future actor for many years. After years of fame as an actor, Fonda still considered Nebraska to be his true home. In fact, on many coast-to-coast flights, he made it a point to stop off for a visit to talk over old times with friends and relatives. His attitude and beliefs (his mother was a practicing Christian Scientist) were those Henry Fonda took from this little town on the prairie shortly after the turn of the century. His parents' stories were almost literally embedded in his bones. The Fondas would move to Omaha in early 1906.

THE HOUSE

Henry Fonda in the bedroom of the Fonda cottage
(Jack Bailey Studio)

THIS PLACE IN ALL ITS SEASONS

The Fondas and a friend of the children's at home in Omaha. Henry is standing between his parents. (Harriet Fonda Warren)

The Fondas in Omaha. Henry is in the center. (Harriet Fonda Warren)

THE HENRY FONDA I KNOW

I never personally met Henry Fonda, but he has touched my life in a hundred ways. He has brought to my life a special purpose. In the beginning, it was the movies I saw. Growing up in the Dust Bowl days, I could relate to the *Grapes of Wrath*, in which he played Tom Joad. I've seen nearly all of Henry's films, but my favorite is *On Golden Pond*. When he received the Academy Award, I cried. I live on Division Street in Grand Island, Nebraska, seven blocks from where Henry Fonda was born. It makes us neighbors of sorts. Perhaps his parents pushed his baby buggy on my sidewalk. I watched the little house where Henry was born being moved from my street to the new Railroad Town site at the Stuhr Museum. My husband and I were at the ground-breaking of the museum, so we were most pleased when Henry was interested enough to provide the funds to move the house to Railroad Town and restore it. After that, driving down our street was never quite the same. The little house was missed. On visits to the museum, it was that little Fonda cottage that tugged at my heartstrings.

So it was, in 1984, I had an idea that, by using my contacts with national magazines and newspapers, I just might do something of special interest to draw attention to this little house.

It was getting close to Christmas, so I asked Jack Learned, the museum's director, for permission to put up a Christmas tree in the little cottage and see what might happen. To make the event meaningful, I contacted Henry's son, Peter, and Peter's wife, Becky, in Montana, to ask if Peter remembered any special Christmas tradition that Henry shared with his children. Through Becky I learned, yes, there was something Henry always did that involved the Christmas tree. It was always his special gift. Henry would put up the tree the night before Christmas. After the children were in bed, he would spend half the night decorating the tree, perhaps with the help of his pal, Jimmy Stewart. The finishing touch was to whip up a mixture of Ivory Snow flakes with a little bit of water, which made a paste-like substance and, together, they would paint the tree to look like it was covered in new fallen snow. Peter noted, "If Henry happened to be working, Christmas just had to wait until he could do the tree!"

I presented the idea to Chris Olson, who wrote for the *Omaha World-Herald*, and the story, complete with photos of the tree, made the newspaper's Sunday edition that Christmas. For the story, Chris interviewed Henry's sister, Mrs. Harriet Warren, in Omaha, about her childhood Christmases. "Our family always celebrated in a traditional fashion," she told him. "We always had a Christmas tree with candles and we always waited until Christmas morning to open up our presents. We had to be dressed and through with breakfast before we could open a single present." Dolls, doll beds, and drums were typical presents in the Fonda household, but Mrs. Warren said she especially remembered the Christmas her father, William Brace Fonda, made a sled for the children. "We lived on California Street in Omaha, and we slid down Happy Hollow Boulevard on that sled. Of course, kids can't do that today because of the traffic."

Decorating the tree in the Henry Fonda cottage with its Fonda tradition was a labor of love that Christmas. We are proud of Henry Fonda's Grand Island roots and that Christmas tree in the kitchen of his cottage symbolized our pride in sharing that with Nebraskans. That first tree also was the beginning of a growing affection for the Fonda family, especially Becky and Peter, who became my dearest friends. I am so lucky!

In 1987, I was given another opportunity, this time to attempt to reproduce and interpret the artifacts and events in the everyday life of the young William Brace Fonda family when they lived in their Grand Island home. The results: a guitar leans against the side of the piano for William to accompany Herberta on the piano. Nearby is a boater straw hat like those William wore. A picnic basket and croquet set are ready for the Fonda family who enjoyed picnics and perhaps a horse and buggy ride to Shimmer's Lake. In the nursery, I added pictures, toys, a baby dress, and hand-hemmed diapers like the ones Herberta might have sewn. A bowl of lemons on the kitchen table and tomatoes ripening on the windowsill could have inspired Henry in his adult life to paint his famous still-life of a bowl of fruit. My favorite room in the cottage is the bedroom where I created a romantic mood with a nightgown casually tossed across the bed, appliquèd quilts, and plump pillows, and the white summer dresses that Herberta favored.

The cottage remains essentially the same today as when the Fonda family lived there—four rooms, a bathroom, nursery, and a little pantry. Coming in off the front porch, you enter a small hallway that leads to the parlor, then on into the dining room. To the left of the hallway is the bedroom, leading to the bathroom and the kitchen. Off the kitchen, is the nursery and pantry. "A sweet little house," as actress Eva Marie Saint once spoke of it after filming there.

The Christmas tree story in the *World-Herald* that year ignited the idea of creating "An Old-Fashioned Christmas" as a special annual winter event at the Railroad Town. The whole museum town is now decorated each year, and completed with carolers and Santa Claus. Each Christmas, four generations of Fonda family traditions, including the snow-covered tree, set the scene in the Fonda cottage. Guests look forward to the year's Christmas card, signed by the Fonda family members when they are usually all together at Thanksgiving. The Christmas card that caused the most excitement in Grand Island was the year that Ted Turner (Jane Fonda's husband) added his name. That made front-page news.

Christmas Tree at Fonda cottage
(Jessie Walker)

The Fonda cottage at the Stuhr Museum decorated for Christmas.
(Jessie Walker)

THIS PLACE IN ALL ITS SEASONS

Young members of the Friends of Henry Fonda
apply Henry's special soapflake "snow" to the Christmas tree.

THE WILLIAM BRACE FONDAS TRAVEL WEST

Ten Eyck Fonda came west to Omaha with his wife Harriet after the Civil War to become chief ticket agent for the Burlington Railroad. This is where his son, William Brace Fonda, was born. The 1899 records show William still lived with his parents at 608 S. 35th Ave. and worked as a clerk for Swift and Co. In 1903, after their marriage, Herberta and William moved farther west to Grand Island, where he was a salesman for the Uneeda Biscuit Co. Here, on May 16, 1905, their son was born. William moved his family back to Omaha in late 1905 or early 1906 and, with hard work, started his own printing business. They first lived at 4709 Cass Street. in Dundee, but as the family grew with the arrival of Henry's sisters, Harriet and Jane, they lived in a succession of homes reflecting their increasing affluence. The family eventually settled in a large house on Chicago Street in one of Omaha's better neighborhoods.

Hard-working and industrious, William Brace was remembered by his son Henry as strict and very self-disciplined, sort of an eccentric man—one of the Liberal

THIS PLACE IN ALL ITS SEASONS

Democrats. The son of a man who had run away from home at the age of seventeen to fight with the Union forces in the Civil War, he did not give in to emotions easily. He liked to fly kites on Sundays. After Henry became a success, he was asked to make a personal contribution to a selection of readings about fathers. He said, "Fathers are eight feet tall and walk with giant steps. I knew my father was the best kite flyer ever."

When Henry was in his early teens, an incident happened that remained with him forever. When W.B. Fonda came home from his plant, dinner would be served and the whole family would exchange small talk. When the meal was over, they would all adjourn to the living room where William would read the newspaper or play the guitar until the children's bedtime rolled around. However, on this particular night, Henry's father arrived home with disturbing news. Talk of it occupied the entire dinner hour. Across the way from the Fonda print shop stood the courthouse. Sometime earlier, in mid-morning, a young black man had been accused of rape. He'd been hunted down, arrested, and kept in the temporary jail in the courthouse. By late afternoon, a large crowd of men had gathered. They were angry and very unruly. When the family finished eating, William Fonda stood up and said, "Henry, I want you to come with me." The two climbed into the car and drove to the plant. They got out and mounted the stairs to the second floor. Henry had always been there when the lights were on, the machinery hummed, and men did their work. Now, however, the room remained dark, the presses were silent, and no one was around. Henry noticed his father's old wooden roll top desk was closed. He could smell the ink and benzene. It was frightening as he sensed the eerie shadows from the lights of the torches held by the men in the crowd below. Even ordinary citizens seemed to be out of control.

Henry's father called him over to the window. The mob screamed for the alleged rapist's blood. No charges had been filed, no grand jury action taken, but the shouts grew louder and louder. Now the mayor, the sheriff, and a few aides pushed through the crowd. Some were on horseback, attempting to quiet the mob. At last, the door to the courthouse opened and a small group of heavily armed men pulled the black man out. Soon the job was done. Henry remembered the next part well. "They took him, strung him up to the end of a lamp post, and hung him and riddled his body with bullets. Then they cut down the body, tied it to the back of an auto, and dragged it through the streets of Omaha. Aside from the lynching, there was something else. My father never said a word. He didn't make a point. He just made sure I saw it."

W.B. Fonda died in 1935 at the age of 56.

From his autobiography *Fonda My Life*, Henry Fonda writes, "My whole damn family was nice. I don't think I've imagined it. It's true. No one could have nicer sisters. No sibling rivalry there.

"Maybe it has to do with being brought up as a Christian Scientist. Half of my relatives were Readers or Practitioners in the church. If you got sick, you sent for Granny or Aunt Bess or Aunt Ethelyn and they'd come and read Mary Baker Eddy to you and you'd get well. We didn't need doctors."

THIS PLACE IN ALL ITS SEASONS

Hattie Brace Fonda, Henry's paternal grandmother. (Sue Fonda)

Ten Eyck Fonda, Henry's paternal grandfather. (Sue Fonda)

HALEY'S COMET

When he was five years old, Henry remembered being awakened by his mother. "I want to show you something, but be real quiet," she said. "We don't want to awaken the girls and your father is tired. He works too hard to lose his sleep." She took his hand in hers and walked down the stairs to the landing.

"A window faced west," Fonda said. "And we looked out and saw this long light streaking across the sky, 10 or 15 degrees above the horizon." His mother put her arm around him and said, "Remember this—Haley's Comet. It comes around only every 76 years. Now remember it." And he always did.

"Gentleness was a quality my parents shared," Fonda said. "They both stood tall. They had attractive features and like so many who are married for a long time, they resembled each other. Father was dark-skinned and mother fair."

From another of his early memories, Fonda recalled, "Dad and Mother would walk three or four blocks to the drug store to get ice cream sodas after we kids had been put to bed. Then they'd walk home. The girls would be asleep, but there was this rhythm in their footsteps on the wooden boards, faintly at first, then nearer and nearer and louder and louder, as they got toward the house. When they started up the steps, I'd nod off."

While making the film *The Farmer Takes a Wife*, Fonda learned of his mother's sudden death. Herberta Fonda had fallen, broken her leg, and developed a blood clot that had traveled to her heart and ended her life. It was 1934 and she was only fifty-five years old.

THE FONDAS IN GRAND ISLAND

From all indications, William Brace and Herberta Fonda were a very intelligent, out-going, and popular couple. After their wedding on June 10, 1903 at the Church of the Good Shepherd in Omaha, the happy newlyweds headed west and settled down in the bustling city of Grand Island, staying at the Palmer House Hotel.

While living at the Palmer House, a February 19, 1904 item appeared in the local newspaper: "Mrs. Fonda taught a very interesting class in the art of cooking at the A.O.U.W. this afternoon at which a number of ladies were present. Mrs. Fonda is a resident in the city and is interested in seeing the best results in the culinary department."

From the May 13, 1904, *Grand Island Independent*: "W.B. Fonda has decided to go into housekeeping and accordingly he has procured a residence on West Division Street, where he and his family will be at home to their friends."

It was in this house a baby boy was born who would carry on the family name as Henry Jaynes Fonda. His birth certificate lists his father as a printer and salesman, born in Omaha. His mother, a "housewife of three years," has her birthplace listed as Wisconsin in 1874. The new parents were both twenty-six years old.

The family would move back to Omaha sometime after December 26, 1905—the day Henry was baptized at St. Stephen's Episcopal Church. His Uncle Ten Eyck Fonda, Jr. and Aunt Ethelon Fonda were there to witness the occasion. The last news item to appear in the *Grand Island Independent* would be on July 28, 1906: "Mrs. W.B. Fonda and her sister, Miss Irene Jaynes, of Omaha are visiting in the city with the families of Thomas Connor and Dr. Roeder." Hopefully they brought the baby.

Herberta Jaynes Fonda

Herberta Jaynes' father, Henry S. Jaynes, a sensitive and cultured man who wrote poetry, was with the Burlington Railroad and has been credited with fostering young Henry Fonda's artistic talents. Her mother's maiden name was Elma Louise Lanphear. They lived in Omaha where Herberta grew up and attended the University of Nebraska. After two years, she went to the Quad Institute in Massachusetts, a Christian Science school.

THE FONDAS IN GRAND ISLAND

WHEN THIS COPY CARRIES THE RAISED SEAL OF THE NEBRASKA HEALTH AND HUMAN SERVICES SYSTEM, IT CERTIFIES THE BELOW TO BE A TRUE COPY OF THE ORIGINAL RECORD ON FILE WITH THE NEBRASKA HEALTH AND HUMAN SERVICES SYSTEM, VITAL STATISTICS SECTION, WHICH IS THE LEGAL DEPOSITORY FOR VITAL RECORDS.

DATE OF ISSUANCE
OCT 2 8 1997

LINCOLN, NEBRASKA

Stanley S. Cooper
STANLEY S. COOPER
ASSISTANT STATE REGISTRAR
HEALTH AND HUMAN SERVICES SYSTEM

F-530

Form 241
State of Nebraska
Department of Public Welfare
BUREAU OF HEALTH—DIVISION OF VITAL STATISTICS

CERTIFICATE OF BIRTH

Do not write in this space
10874

1. PLACE OF BIRTH
County __Hall__
Township _____
City __Grand Island__ Street __620 - West Division St.__

DECEASED

{If birth occurred in a hospital or institution give its NAME instead of street and number.}

2. FULL NAME OF CHILD __Henry Jaynes Fonda__

3. Sex __Male__ | If plural births | 4. Twin, triplet, or other ____ | 6. Premature ____ | 7. Legitimate? __Yes__ | 8. Date of birth __May 16th__ 1905
5. Number, in order of birth ____ | Full term __Yes__ | (Month, day, year)

9. Full name FATHER	18. Full maiden name MOTHER
William Brace Fonda	Herberta Jaynes
10. Post Office Grand Island, Neb.	19. Post Office Grand Island, Neb.
11. Color or race White	12. Age at last birthday 26 (Years)	20. Color or race White	21. Age at last birthday 26 (Years)
13. Birthplace (city or place) Omaha (State or country) Nebraska	22. Birthplace (city or place) Wisconsin (State or country)
14. Trade, profession, or particular kind of work done, as spinner, sawyer, bookkeeper, etc. Salesman	23. Trade, profession, or particular kind of work done, as housekeeper, typist, nurse, clerk, etc. House-Keeper
15. Industry or business in which work was done, as silk mill, sawmill, bank, etc. Printing	24. Industry or business in which work was done, as own home, lawyer's office, silk mill, etc. at own home
16. Date (mo. and yr.) last engaged in this work May 16 1905	17. Total time (years) spent in this work 5	25. Date (mo. and yr.) last engaged in this work May 16 1923	26. Total time (years) spent in this work 3

27. Number of children of this mother (At time of this birth and including this child) (a) Born alive and now living __One__ (b) Born alive but now dead __0__ (c) Stillborn __0__

28. If stillborn, period of gestation ____ {months or weeks} 29. Cause of stillbirth ____ {Before labor ____ / During labor ____}

CERTIFICATE OF ATTENDING PHYSICIAN *

I hereby certify that I attended the birth of this child, who was __born alive__ at ____ A.M. on the date above stated.
(Born alive) (Stillborn)

* When no physician is in attendance certificate shall be completed and signed by the parent or other person present.

Signature __George Roeder__ M.D.
Address __Grand Island, Neb.__

STATE LAW
Was silver solution instilled in each eye? __Yes__
Filed with local registrar __AUG 7 1929__
Date

__H E Clifford__
Registrar

THIS PLACE IN ALL ITS SEASONS

Henry with his maternal grandfather Henry Jaynes.
(Harriet Fonda Warren)

Left to right Herberta Jaynes Fonda, her mother Alma Lanphear
Jaynes, and grandmother Myra Louise Lanphear
and Henry and Harriet. (Harriet Fonda Warren)

WHAT MIGHT HAVE BEEN...
AND WHAT WAS

*I*f Henry Fonda had grown up in Grand Island, Nebraska, it's possible he might have become a movie star, but it is doubtful. I don't believe there would have been many opportunities to inspire him. But I'm quite sure that whatever he would have set out to do, he would have been very successful.

As he speaks of his youth in his biography, Henry Fonda could have certainly played ball, cops and robbers, cowboys and Indians with the neighborhood kids. In the winter, there were many places to toboggan, make snowmen, and have snowball fights. He certainly could have become an Eagle Scout as he did in Omaha. He probably could have won a short story contest and maybe even worked for the *Grand Island Independent*. He certainly could have graduated in 1923 from Grand Island Senior High School and gone on to college for journalism studies. His father, W.B. Fonda, was a good provider and, no doubt, as the family grew to five, would have possibly bought a larger house farther west in the growing area of Division, Koenig, and Charles Streets.

However, we know while Henry was still in diapers, the family moved to Omaha; a move that would change the course of his life and that of his own family.

While Jane Fonda and I were standing together in the hallway of Walnut Junior High School awaiting entrance to Peter Fonda's workshop on Henry Fonda Day in August 1992, I said to Jane, "It certainly makes a difference who your father is, doesn't it?" She looked at me, and without hesitation, replied, "It sure does!" Henry Jaynes Fonda may have had his first press notice in the Grand Island paper when he was born and spent his first months in Grand Island, but it would take Omaha and the Omaha Community Playhouse and a phone call from Do Brando to make this day in Grand Island come about these many years later.

AT THE OMAHA COMMUNITY PLAYHOUSE

I have attended performances at the Omaha Community Playhouse. I have sat in the honored Henry Fonda chair in the Fonda-McGuire Theater section of the Playhouse and, one afternoon, I sat in the theater watching sets being built and lights being installed for an upcoming production. You get the feeling something special is happening. I could imagine Henry doing this back in his first years of theater.

Although Grand Island is proud of Henry's first home and where he was born, it is Omaha that claims his youth and his interest in the theater, which Henry said back then was only his hobby and would not become his career. He graduated from Central High School in Omaha, where he had been interested in athletics, art, and writing, and went on to the University of Minnesota the following two years to earn a degree in journalism. The pressure of schoolwork and long hours of working two jobs soon forced the exhausted twenty-year-old to return to his family in Omaha. Short on experience, he was unable to find steady employment, so when the opportunity for full-time work arrived, he took it—even if it wasn't exactly what he had in mind.

At the insistence of his mother's friend, Do Brando, Marlon Brando's mother, Henry tried out for a role in an upcoming Playhouse production. Reluctantly, Fonda agreed to read a part in Philip Barry's comedy, *You and I* and won the role. He did well and discovered the theater. The rest of the season was spent building and painting scenery, applying make-up, and appearing in minor roles. His growing interest in acting received little interest or encouragement at home. Both of his parents, hoping their son would find respectable employment, were relieved when Henry landed a job as an office boy at the end of the season.

In preparing for the next new season at the Playhouse, the director suggested a role that was ideal for the young actor. The play was *Merton of the Movies*, which, oddly enough, was the story of a small town clerk who dreams of becoming a Hollywood star. He accepted the part against his father's wishes. He could live at home, his parents agreed, if he promised not to quit his $18 a week job at the Retail Credit Office. Working during the day and rehearsing at night, Fonda enthusiastically accepted the challenge of his first major role. His opening night performance was met with thunderous applause. It was a memorable night in his professional career. The famous story goes that even his stubborn father was won over by his performance. When Henry's sister Harriet voiced a critical comment, the family's reticent W.B. Fonda came to his son's defense: "Shut up," he admonished from behind the evening paper. "He was perfect."

Until now, Henry looked on acting as a hobby, but when Foley of the Playhouse offered him $500 a year for the position of assistant director of the Playhouse, he jumped at the opportunity. Soon he was appearing opposite Do Brando in Eugene O'Neill's *Beyond the Horizon* and, during the summer, he toured the Midwest with Lincoln impressionist George Billings. There would be another season at the Playhouse, but it would be Fonda's last. By now, everyone knew the actor's talents were destined to be shared. He would head for New York and Cape Cod.

NEW YORK AND CAPE COD

I was in New York City in the 1970s when Henry Fonda was playing on Broadway. Reading the *New York Times* in my hotel room, I saw the opportunity to see him perform. However, I was there alone on business and, even though I wanted to go, I could not get up the nerve to go to the theater by myself. If I were to do it over, knowing my interest now, that would have been first on my list.

Just last summer, my daughter and I drove up from Boston to Cape Cod and made a visit to the Cape Playhouse in Denis, Massachusetts. I wanted to go there and feel the sand beneath my feet that Henry and Margaret Sullivan enjoyed together, and just see the Playhouse.

To me, it was all that I expected, very clapboard, New England, and summer stock. I was pleased to tell the sales clerk in the gift shop that I was from Grand Island, Nebraska, where Henry Fonda was born, and about how the house where he was born is decorated at the Stuhr Museum, and that I was friends with Peter and Becky Fonda. It made me very proud and she, in turn, was anxious to visit Nebraska and especially Grand Island and Omaha to see where it really began.

LETTER TO DAD

The Hollywood part of Henry Fonda's life I have left for the biographers. It has been documented time and time again. However, I would like to include part of his letter written to his father in Omaha while making *Way Down East* very early in his film career.

>August 1935
>
>Dear Dad,
>   Had the afternoon off yesterday and celebrated by buying a new car—maybe it's better I should keep busy.
>   But I got a good deal—they allowed me $325 for my 1932 convertible coupe that I paid $400 for in February—and so the new job—same style cost me $562 with radio.
>   It is a honey. I really owed it to myself—the old job was getting pretty noisy and had a habit of stalling in the middle of impatient traffic.
>   And I got a Scotty pup—brother to Sullivan's pups—just seven weeks old—with

champions way back on both sides. His father's name was Boy of Sleat—so he naturally becomes "Boy."

On the way home tonight I bought a pair of Strawberry Finches—a pair of Japanese Rice birds—for my aviary.

And the ant exterminator man has been here all day making his own racket—and we expect to be much happier. A couple of them were carrying away a tennis ball this morning when I came out to breakfast.

Love,
Henry

Shared by Mary Shanley, Henry Fonda's niece

ELIZA SONNELAND CLARK WALKS WITH HENRY FONDA

There are people still living in Grand Island who have family stories to tell of Henry Fonda when he was a baby and of happenings then.

Here is one of my favorite ones as told by Eliza Sonneland Clark, who now lives in Texas, for the Friends of Henry Fonda Newsletter.

The year, the theater, even the season are long gone from memory. But not the moment itself.

Every child grows up with stories of "I knew him when…" And one that had been bandied about in my house was the fact that my grandmother, Irma "Nanny" Woolstenholm Sonneland, had pushed the baby carriage of Henry Fonda back in Grand Island, Nebraska. It was a neat piece of information to pass on as the opportunity to do so presented itself.

Flash forward to mid- to late-70s. I'm a student at the Neighborhood Playhouse School of Theater in New York City by day. By night, I'm bartending in Broadway theaters. It was a terrific job for an aspiring actress, especially because I had the opportunity to see so many shows free! I can't count the number of times I saw *Sweeny Todd*.

Anyway, one of my assignments took me to *The First Monday in October* starring Henry Fonda and Jane Alexander. A not-bad play about the Supreme Court taking on its first woman justice, or "Justess" as Mr. Fonda's character referred to Ms. Alexander. I remember the theater being the type that required actors to walk down a long alley to get to the stage door. (The Winter Garden, maybe?) Since we acting wannabees took every opportunity to rub elbows with the real thing, I figured I could use the "My grandmother pushed your baby carriage…" story to start a conversation with Mr. Fonda.

So there I was, planning my strategy as I headed into work when I realized the guy in front of me, about to turn down the alley, was none other than…yep, the big Mr. F.

Okay, here goes… "Excuse me, Mr. Fonda?" I'll never forget the expression that came from this man's back. In a millisecond, I caught the "Oh, no, please don't be some nutty fan bent on accosting me." Since I didn't consider myself some nutty fan, I pressed on. "Mr. Fonda, I just wanted to say Hi. I work at this theater… and I wanted to tell you that my grandmother used to push your baby carriage in Grand Island, Nebraska!" By this time, we were walking shoulder to shoulder. He stopped in his tracks, looked at me, and broke into a smile and then into a laugh. "Grand Island, Nebraska!"

We continued down the alley, the rest of the conversation now long forgotten. And I'm left with a memory, not just of a handed-down family story about a movie star and a baby carriage, but a man enjoying the memory of Grand Island, Nebraska.

OMAHA PLAYHOUSE HONORS HENRY FONDA

On January 15, 1981, at the age of 75, Henry Fonda went back to Omaha one last time. The Omaha Community Playhouse was throwing a party for him that they called "An Evening with Mr. Fonda." It began with a reception for 500 people, followed by a two-hour film tribute, and then Henry went on stage to visit and answer questions. He told the audience, "None of this would have happened without the training I received at the Playhouse," where he first acted. "I really feel that I was a lucky boy to grow up in Omaha," he added. He talked of his years at Central High School, where he was painfully self-conscious partially because he was so short. "My cadet uniform in my senior year wouldn't fit my grandson today."

His publicist, John Springer, and host for the evening had put together and narrated a film retrospective of Fonda's work dating back to 1931 when he was a member of the University Players doing summer stock on the East Coast. In a film interview, Jane Fonda spoke of the simplicity of her father's tastes, saying, "I sometimes think he was better suited to run a bookstore in Omaha." Springer also introduced Henry's sister, Harriet Warren of Omaha; cousins Mr. and Mrs. Douw Fonda, of Denver; director Joshua Logan; Peter Fonda and his then wife, Portia; Henry's fifth wife, Shirlee; and actress Dorothy McGuire, another Playhouse graduate. Henry Fonda surprised Miss McGuire by calling her up to the stage to discover the Playhouse had put her name on a chair in the theater—a symbolic tribute that is the Playhouse's highest honor. Only ten others, including Fonda, have chairs.

One question asked of Fonda by a twelve-year-old girl for her school newspaper was, "What is the key to happiness?" The actor thought for a second. "Know how to cook well, know the name of a good doctor who makes house calls, and make good friends." At the end of the question and answer session, Fonda called fourteen-year-old grandson, Justin Fonda, to the stage. He noted that Jane and Peter had all begun their careers in Playhouse productions, and said, "I just want you to see what's hanging around in the wings. I thought it might be appropriate that Justin take his first bow at the Omaha Community Playhouse."

The last question that night was asked by Peter Fonda: "Mr. Fonda, this is your son," he said. "We've really enjoyed this evening with you Mr. Fonda, and we were just wondering, would it be possible for us to have dinner with you now?"

From the Sun Newspapers of Omaha

"The entire evening was filled with emotionally moving moments. When the applauding was over and the house lights dimmed, all left that evening in one warm, rosy glow. Omaha had honored Henry Fonda on that one night, but everyone was aware that Henry had been honoring Omaha for years."

OMAHA PLAYHOUSE HONORS HENRY FONDA

From Fred Teller, retired manager and theater owner of Hastings, Nebraska.

My favorite story is about the road company of *Mister Roberts*, starring Henry Fonda, which was booked at the Omaha Theatre for four performances in March 1951. It was sold out for all four performances in a 2,000-seat house. The show played in Minneapolis the week before Omaha. The show closed on Saturday and the troupe was to travel to Omaha by train Sunday, but fate stepped in with the biggest snowstorm of the season. The train stalled near Siley, Iowa, halfway to Omaha. There were two shows scheduled for Monday. Late Monday night, Fonda called the theater. He had trekked the better part of a mile through snowdrifts. He was concerned about his Omaha family and asked them to call his sister to let her know he was all right. He also was concerned about the 2,000 who had tickets for the Monday presentation. The train finally arrived about 4 P.M. Tuesday. There was no time to set scenery and hang the show by 6:30 P.M. They were only able to get the costumes off the train and, that evening before a full house, Henry Fonda came on stage as Mister Roberts and said: "If you are going to make theater history, you might as well do it in your hometown."

He set the stage by telling the audience exactly where everything was supposed to be. "This is Mister Roberts' quarters. Here is the captain's table, the hatch, the gun mounts..."

Then, he proceeded to lead two great performances of *Mister Roberts* on a bare stage with the brick back wall in full view. Following the performance on this exhausting night, Mr. Fonda graciously attended a reception at the Omaha Community Playhouse in his honor.

A VISIT WITH EVA MARIE SAINT

*I*t was the last day of the filming of *My Antonia* in Railroad Town at the Stuhr Museum. Actress Eva Marie Saint had just finished a scene near the Henry Fonda birthplace cottage. She was headed for lunch and a noon break when I caught up with her. Without missing a step, we made arrangements for a telephone interview. She promised to call. At quarter till five, I picked up the phone on its first ring. She only had a minute.

"It's been such an honor to work in the sweet little house that Henry was born in," she said. "I enjoyed my stay here, but found the tornado weather very frightening. Wonderful drivers though, but it was very scary. Nothing like it in California. The museum is wonderful. The exhibits are like sculptures. I would compare it to the Kennedy Center in Washington, D.C., with the Potomac River in the background. And out here is this miniature in Nebraska with the moat surrounding it.

"My husband came out on Fourth of July weekend and we drove to Red Cloud, Nebraska. You know, I was their honored speaker there a few years ago."

"Yes, I know," I replied "I was there."

The actress spoke of the land and the people in Nebraska as very "genuine and nice. I especially notice families laughing and eating together…and mothers with their children. It is so refreshing to see that. Different in California." She glowingly spoke of our beautiful countryside out where she had been filming near Bolus, Nebraska.

"I hope to return someday soon, especially to Red Cloud, and play Willa Cather. We have talked about it. Will you come? I'm sorry to have to hang up, but I must go now to meet the governor. Then I will catch the flight for home and California."

"Aren't I lucky?" I thought as I hung up the phone. This little house has connected me with one of Henry's acting colleagues who was also his good friend.

CATCHING UP WITH DAVID RINTELS

The *Grand Island Daily Independent* ran an article about producer David Rintels and his wife Victoria Risken Rintels. They were interviewed on location in Railroad Town at the Stuhr Museum where they were filming *My Antonia*. Rintels was quoted in the article as saying, "Getting the opportunity to be in Henry Fonda's home was a highlight of my Grand Island stay. This is something very special."

That's all it took! I called his hotel and left a message on his answering machine, plus I wrote a note and with several Friends of Henry Fonda newsletters in a large brown envelope and dropped them off at his mailbox. Then I waited.

A call came about 10:20 that night. The voice was direct, "This is David Rintels." I was delighted! We agreed to meet on the set the following day. "Anytime; they will know where to find me." I choose noon. At the conclusion of our visit, David asked that I send him a copy of our newsletter containing the interview. Following is the note he wrote to me after reading the fall issue with the first part of the interview.

CATCHING UP WITH DAVID RINTELS

Dear Ruth:

Thanks for the newsletter! I love it (but who wouldn't love it, seeing his own words quoted back to him).

...The show my wife and I did in Grand Island, *My Antonia*, will be on USA Cable in later March. I hope you see it.

I saw Jane F. a couple of months ago in Georgia—I wrote and produced a show for Ted Turner on ANDERSONVILLE and they came on the set—she looks great (and is great).

Thanks for the pictures—I'm very glad to have them. With luck I'll see you soon.

Best, David

STORIES OF FONDA
An Interview with David Rintels

I interviewed David Rintels, motion picture producer and director of *My Antonia*, filmed at the Stuhr Museum in Grand Island, Nebraska. Mr. Rintels had worked with and known Henry Fonda both in his professional and personal life. The interview not only gives us new insight into Henry Fonda, but we also find David Rintels to be a fine storyteller.

I met Henry, who wished to be called "Hank," in 1973, after I had written a play on Clarence Darrow. The producer had sent a copy of the play to Henry and he wanted to do it. We went into rehearsals that year and Henry had great success with that play.

Something I always remember…The play *Clarence Darrow* opens with Darrow talking about something his father had told him. When Darrow was seven, eight, or nine years old, there was a hanging in the town where Rintels was raised in Ohio. And Darrow's father told him that, like everyone else in the town, he went down to see this hanging.

It was a big event. But just at the moment of the hanging, he turned his head away and he felt humiliated and ashamed for the rest of his life that he had that much to do with the taking of a man's life, even just being there. And that was Darrow's father speaking to Darrow and it influenced Clarence Darrow who became a very strong opponent of capital punishment. Well, Fonda told me that when he read the play, his father told him of a similar story: that there was a lynching in the town where they were [Omaha]... Fonda's father told him how he had hated it and it made a strong impression on him. It impressed Fonda tremendously that his experience with his own father was similar to Darrow's experience with his father. It touched him.

There's something else that I saw happen time after time in *Clarence Darrow* that always touched me. When the play opens, Hank, playing Darrow, would come out, and the audience would always give him a warm round of applause. They loved and respected him even before he opened his mouth. The way the play is constructed, there are three sets on the stage: there's his office, the courtroom, and his apartment or his home. And he spends a moment walking among them—just sort of remembering things, thinking about his life. And then he comes downstage and he relates the story about his father telling of the hanging and the first words of the play are, "When I was very young..." And you would see a wonderful thing happen in the audience; people would just sort of relax. They would sit back. They knew that, somehow, they were in good hands—that here was something that was uniquely American; that Henry Fonda was about to take them back to another time and place. And it didn't matter anymore if it was Darrow or Fonda. It was just a time when America was an easier place to live. You knew that you would be OK, and for two hours you were.

In 1975, I guess, Hank did something he had always wanted to do and had never done. He went to do the play

Darrow in London. He had never acted on the London stage, and even Jimmy Stewart was there. I'll tell you something about that night I don't think has ever been printed. It's customary for a star on an opening night of a play in London to give a curtain call where he says something to the audience. And Hank was embarrassed. He didn't want to do it. He was uncomfortable. But here was this big round of applause and everyone kept pushing him. "You gotta do it, you gotta go out there." And so finally he did. And he comes out and says "Well, I've always wanted to do this and now I have." They went crazy.

I loved him [Hank]. He was really kind to me. When I met him, I was writing episodes of television shows. I didn't have a dream that the best actor in America would take my first play to Broadway. That was something. In 1979 or 1980, we were making a film of *Gideon's Trumpet*. Clarence Earl Gideon was the name of the character and Henry played him. Gideon was a drifter; a man who had never amounted to very much, and he gets arrested for some petty crime. When he is brought to court, he asks the court to give him a lawyer. "Just because I can't afford one, you should get me one." And the judges tell him no. So Gideon appeals to the Supreme Court and, miracle of miracles, they agree to hear his case. It became a famous court case. It was decided in the early 1960s and the Supreme Court stated that no American should have to be put on trial without a lawyer ever again. If he can't afford one, then the state has to pay for it. And that was the origin of the public defender. Some states had done it, but never the whole nation. And Fonda played that character. My wife's mother, Faye Wray, was in it and so were John Houseman, Jose Ferrar, Sam Jaffe, and Dean Jaegger. We had a great cast.

When we would break for lunch...You work in our business six hours and then the director hollers "Lunch! 30 minutes." Everybody runs for the food wagon. Customarily, the stars go the head of the line. Hank would never do that. He would stand in line and take his turn like everybody else. The crew loved him for that.

We were doing shots of Fonda and the jury. You know how it works in the movie business where you would put a camera behind the jury and photograph Fonda, or put a camera behind Fonda and photograph the jury. There were also shots where you put the camera in the place where Fonda was and the camera would have Henry Fonda's point of view. It came time to do Henry Fonda's point of view. The director said to Mr. Fonda, "You're not in this shot and you don't have to read your lines behind the camera." Henry said, "Oh, no. When I spoke to them, they gave my the courtesy to listen to me and I'm going to do the same for them." These were twelve extras. These weren't actors that had speaking lines. Most actors would have been off in their dressing rooms, but not Henry Fonda. He was a professional. Hank always knew that his strength and his limitations as an actor were that he was purely American. He knew he couldn't do Shakespeare. Didn't want to do Shakespeare. If they wanted him to do it he'd say get another actor. "That's not what I do."

He told me about the opening night of *Mister Roberts* in New York. That must have been the greatest opening night in the history of the theatre, right up there with whatever you can think of. Hank said at the end of the play there were twenty-two curtain calls and the twenty second was as loud as the first. The audience was standing on their chairs cheering and they didn't know how to end it...how to get the audience out of the theatre. So that is the only other time that Hank spoke of the audience at the end of a play. He comes out and he holds up his hands and he says, "That's all he wrote."

Henry was in *Mister Roberts* over 1700 performances. And after a couple of years, Jimmy Stewart came to see the play and he came backstage afterwards. He said, "Hank, you're fabulous, you're wonderful. But you have been doing it for three straight years without a break. Why don't you take a couple of weeks vacation and I will fill in for you? And Fonda says, "Get away from me you SOB."

He only played the bad guy once in a movie and that was *Once Upon a Time in the West*. He said it was a funny experience, but loved the movie. He said that Sergio Leone came to him and asked him to do the part. The picture opens with Fonda leading a gang who kills some people and there is a little boy who sees them. Because Fonda is afraid this innocent child can identify them, he either kills him or orders him to be killed. That's the way the picture opens. Fonda says to the director, "You can't cast me for this. People are going to look into these baby blues...that's not the thing I do." The director says, "No, no that's exactly why I want you to do this. It will be so unexpected that you won't look like the kind of guy who would do that."

We went to visit him on the set of *On Golden Pond* and I thought he was in pretty good shape. He was having a very good experience. That picture meant more to him, I think, than any picture he had ever done; for obvious reasons. He was so glad to do it with Jane, and for Jane and for himself. He was doing that the summer of '80 or '81 and it was a great summer for him. That was one of his last summers.

A BIRTHDAY CELEBRATION

The Friends of Henry Fonda and the Stuhr Museum celebrate Henry Fonda's birth with a birthday party in the little green cottage where he was born. Once when my husband and I were in Missouri on a short vacation, we stopped in Lamar, Missouri, to stay overnight. Coming into town, we'd noticed a sign pointing to the Harry Truman birthplace. After checking into our motel, we followed the directions that led to the little house of our 33rd President of the United States.

It was "after hours," so we peeked in windows and were taking pictures when a little girl came over to us. We said, "Hello," and she replied proudly, "We serve cake on his birthday." "You do? What a nice idea," I replied. And that is how another event got started at the little Fonda birthplace at the Stuhr Museum in Grand Island. Now, we serve cake every year on his birthday and we also fly kites.

Henry, himself, loved to fly kites. At the dinner of the Stuhr Museum's Tribute to Henry Fonda, Henry's son, Peter, told the story about his father and actor Jimmy Stewart putting together a kite, and he reminisced about his father flying this very kite for him. A very special kite flies on these

Fonda birthday events. It was made especially for this day by Rupert Cox, another kite flyer and artist who died soon after he built and flew it. Since then, his son, Eric, comes out from Omaha for Henry's birthday event to fly his father's Henry Fonda kite. Other fellow kite flyers are invited to fly their kites.

Also included for the event is a statewide art contest for seventh, eighth, and ninth grade students, and a scholarship is given by the Friends of Henry Fonda to a Hall County drama student.

Henry Fonda kite flown by its creator, Rupert Cox.
(Bob McCauley)

A BIRTHDAY CELEBRATION

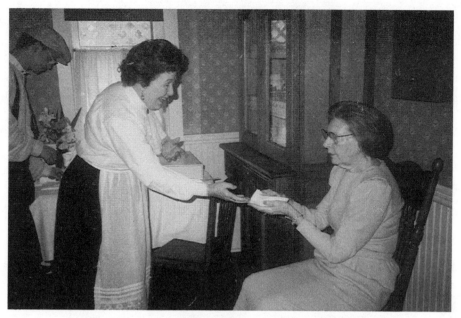

Helen Peterson, a member of the Friends of Henry Fonda, serves birthday cake to Emma Corey.

Friends of Henry Fonda Membership Card.

HALLMARK CHRISTMAS CARD

*I*n a December issue of a popular decorator magazine, I was reading an article about Christmas cards. A section was devoted to some very famous people who had painted them such as Jackie Kennedy Onassis, Winston Churchill, and then there were others done by Hollywood stars, such as Groucho Marx, Fred MacMurray, Jane Wyman, and Henry Fonda. No mention was made of the card companies they had all painted the cards for.

Christmas was coming, and I thought, "Wouldn't it be great if I could locate that card." I called different members of the Fonda family and they did not seem to have any knowledge of it. They did remember that Henry would sometimes send his cards to be postmarked "Fonda, New York." I decided to call Hallmark Inc. I asked for their archives. Presto! "Yes, Henry Fonda painted a card in 1948 for Hallmark. It was part of a box of Hollywood celebrities: Groucho Marx, Fred MacMurray, Jane Wyman, and Henry Fonda."

Fonda's original artwork was returned to the family. The late actor's Christmas card featured colorfully wrapped presents on a table beside a silver plate and three branches of

HALLMARK CHRISTMAS CARD

an evergreen tree decorated with tinsel and a single red ornament. On the plate was a little card that said, "Merry Christmas." They would be happy to make up the card on special heavy parchment paper. "How many do you want?" I asked for six; two for myself and four to send Fonda family members.

Later, I learned from Shirlee Fonda that the original had been stolen and had turned up with other Fonda memorabilia at a New York auction.

An original Hallmark Christmas card by Henry Fonda.
(Hallmark Archives, Hallmark Cards, Inc.)

CHRISTMAS AT THE FONDA COTTAGE, 1995

On a warm, clear, moonlit night, Christmas came again to the little Fonda cottage that once stood on Division Street. The friends of Henry Fonda welcomed a record-breaking crowd, all of whom seemed to be in a festive mood. The house was gift-wrapped with four generations of Fonda family traditions. In the parlor stood the "snow-covered" tree just like Hank would put up the night before Christmas. Underneath, were the toys left by Santa for Jane and the "good boy" Peter. There also was the family's latest photograph. The buffet in the dining room featured a feather tree with antique Dresden ornaments. On the table, as part of the centerpiece, was the annual Christmas greeting from the Fonda family.

On the great hearth stove in the kitchen, we honored Henry Fonda's service to his country in the United States Navy during the 50th anniversary of World War II. In an added display were some of the endearing letters he had written home to his small children and his married sister, Jayne. People seemed transfixed with emotion, both young and old alike, as they took time to read and study them. I noticed tears welling up in some eyes of the older veterans as they turned away. I think we captured insight to Henry Fonda; not as a famous personality or movie star, but as a real, loving father away at war writing tender letters home to his children. His words were solicitous and caring.

Tuesday, 10 October

My Dearest Son,
    I had a letter from Mummy today, and she said that you had been thinking of me and wondering what I was doing. And now I am sitting here and wondering how I can tell you what I am doing. I am thinking about you so much and so often that it never occurs to me to think about you thinking about me.
    When I think about you I always put myself right near you at home. I think about working in the garden and having you work beside me and every now and then you will say to me, "Daddy, I'm a good boy." And when I go down the hill to the stable, you call out to Mackie, "Mackie, I'm going with Daddy!"
    So you see I think of myself as being at home when I think of you and I forget that it must be hard for you to realize how far away I am and what I am doing.
    I am living now on a big ship, and we are anchored in the harbor of an island way across the Pacific Ocean. This island was held by the Japs until a short time ago. I don't mean to give you the impression that I took it away from them by myself. There were quite a few Marines that helped me.

THIS PLACE IN ALL ITS SEASONS

I have a room about as big as your bathroom that I share with another officer, and I sleep in the top bunk of a double-decked bunk like in a Pullman train, but of course you've never been in a train. That's silly.

Most of the walls of the room are covered with pictures of you and Lady and Pan sitting on the blue seat out by the pool. And if I look a little to the right, there you are when you were just a baby, sitting on Mummy's lap with your finger in your mouth and Little Lady is standing behind Mummy playing with her hair and Pan is sitting on the grass beside you patting Mike and just a little more to the right and I can see you leaning over the bars in your play yard, laughing and looking right at me. I can almost hear you say, "Hi Dad!"

And if I listen real carefully I can hear somebody say, "Look what I'm doing, Daddy" and I look over to the left and there is Lady leaning on her bicycle and further over I can see you and Lady sitting on a haystack and if I turn around I could see all of you playing together.

But I won't turn around now or I won't ever finish this letter. I know there is no good in my trying to explain to you why I am away from home. War doesn't make sense even when you are grown up, but I think that someday you will understand why I had to be in it.

It's not natural for a father to be away from his family as long as I have had to be. Ordinarily a boy grows up and has his father right with him all the time, but we are unlucky, because a war had to come along and a

CHRISTMAS AT THE FONDA COTTAGE, 1995

lot of fathers had to go away and a lot of young sons have had to puzzle it out and wonder where Dad went and what he is doing.

I'm not always sure of what I'm doing, but I know why I'm doing it: to get the whole thing over with as soon as possible so that I can come home again and live with my family and watch my children grow up.

Good night, Son. Give Mummy and Lady a big hug and kiss for me and be a good boy.

Dad.

Note: A copy of this letter written in longhand was given to me by the niece of Henry Fonda, Mary Shanely, who is also a Friends of Henry Fonda member.

Christmas decorations in the Fonda cottage
on the 50th anniversary of WWII.

The kitchen stove and view into the nursery.

CHRISTMAS AT THE FONDA COTTAGE, 1995

The bedroom decorated for Christmas.

A CHRISTMAS STORY COMES FULL CIRCLE

From Chris Olsen's 1984 story in the *Omaha World-Herald* about the first Fonda Christmas tree that I created, to 1998, the Fonda Christmas tree story has come full circle—in two different ways. First, in a magazine article in the November-December 1998 publication *Victorian Decorating and Lifestyles*, entitled "Christmas on the Prairie," with a subtitle, "The Memory of a Beloved American Actor Illuminates a Restored Home in Nebraska."

The seven-page article, written by the magazine staff writer Paul Slimak of New York City and illustrated with incredibly beautiful photographs by Jessie Walker of Chicago, a nationally known interiors photographer, tells the complete story of the Fonda birth home, Henry Fonda himself, and Christmas in the cottage. I had presented the idea several years ago and was thrilled to see it all come about.

PETER FONDA REMEMBERS CHRISTMASES

Second, in Peter Fonda's biography, *Don't Tell Dad*, he remembers their Christmas tree was like no one else's in Bel Aire.

"On Christmas morning we would bound downstairs and stop in wonderment as we stared at the incredible Christmas tree, filled with beautiful ornaments, tinsel, garlands, colored lights, and snow. Snow filled every bough, making them droop just like snow-covered trees.

"The surprise of the tree, which had stood barren for the few days before the holidays, had been bestowed by Father Christmas overnight. It was an incredible icon of everything Christmas trees were supposed to be, more exciting than the expectation of our open presents. It was magic, the best present of all, rendered so by our Dad."

Funny how things come around. It was this "Snow on the Christmas Tree" story that Peter, through his wife, Becky, had relayed to me 13 years ago that ultimately brought this book into being.

THE VISIT

Over the years in our visits together, Becky and I had talked how we hoped she, Peter, and Jane could come out to Grand Island to see Henry's house. "Some day," she promised. An unsuccessful attempt was made in 1988 when Jane suddenly had to go to Mexico to make a movie. Also, some premature publicity went out to the press about it and Vietnam War Vets began a protest at the museum. The whole idea was aborted. The seed had been planted, nonetheless. Soon after this, my late husband, Bob, and I took a short trip to the Northwest, which included Montana. Becky had arranged the accommodations for us.

After checking into our motel, I made a phone call for directions to the ranch. "When you come to a beat-up old mail box, you make a left turn," was the first of Becky's instructions. Past fields of hay in the Paradise Valley, surrounded by brooding hills of the Absaraka range with big blue sky overhead, we drove up the long lane to the Fonda ranch house where Becky was waving and motioning us on into the yard. Right behind her were two happy, bounding golden labs, which she would introduce as "my precious babies." What a welcoming committee.

THE VISIT

We were ushered through the garden into the house. Peter, with that great Fonda smile, came out in his bathrobe to say hello. It was morning. Had I been here before? It all looked so familiar—the flower garden we passed through to the house. There was the doorjamb in the kitchen where the children's early growth marks were recorded. A collage of family and friends' photographs covered the refrigerator. There to the west was the window where the snow-decorated Christmas tree stood in the photograph that Becky had sent me after my very first phone call. And there's the phone. On the wall I recognized the Henry Fonda paintings along with those that I would learn were Russell Chatham's. The front screen door opened to the same view Becky had described when a United Parcel Service truck was coming up their lane. In the back was the hill that she and Peter had climbed one night to watch a magnificent solar event. All of these things I recognized from the conversations we had over those miles and miles of telephone wires. That view, and this log house, definitely belonged to the great-great-great-granddaughter of the famous Davy Crockett of Alamo fame and the only son of the movie legend, Henry Fonda.

Peter, so gracious, has a great sense of humor. No wonder one of my girl ancestors, Elizabeth Vanwaught Wilson, fell in love with and married one of Peter's ancestors, James Robert Fonda, son of a Peter and Jennie Caughtry Fonda back in Troy, New York, in November 1840. Peter greatly impressed me way back when he was living in Omaha with his Aunt Harriet, attending the university there. He wrote a letter to the Public Pulse column of the *Omaha World-Herald*. "I love Omaha," he wrote. "I buy my clothes here and people go to the theater, not to be seen, but because they love the theater." We Nebraskans often had a low opinion of ourselves, so when this letter appeared, it was rather reassuring. At the same time, I was writing articles for magazines about our wonderful state, trying to promote it in my own way, and this dear young man, Peter Fonda, had written these few words and said it all so well. "I love Omaha." Wow! He still never misses a Nebraska football game and thinks our Sandhills are spectacular.

It was in the kitchen at the Fonda table, covered with a white crocheted tablecloth, over coffee and Becky's hot-from-the-oven, melt-in-your-mouth biscuits and homemade jelly, that our conversation would finally get around to Henry's house. "Is there anything we can do to get your family out there to see it?" I asked. "The Stuhr Museum would really like to do a special tribute to your father and, of course, we'd want the Fonda family to come." Grand Island is sort of a fly-over city. You either go over it or pass by it on the interstate, ten miles away. Peter's Aunt Harriet lived in Omaha, but we were still 130 miles west. We needed a plan that they would all want to be a part of.

"What about a film festival?" I asked. I had heard the Donna Reed Film Festival in Denison, Iowa, seemed to be doing well. Maybe a Henry Fonda Film Festival? Peter thought a minute. "That takes a lot of work, a real commitment. A film festival that is usually very successful has to have more than just the festival to draw people. It needs a special atmosphere. A location that is popular and fun. The name Henry Fonda Film Festival would not be enough. They go to Robert Redford's Sundance Festival and to the Cannes Film Festival because of their fantastic locations. I just don't think it would work out in Grand Island." He was being honest and I understood completely. I actually had doubted it myself. So for the time being, we just let that idea sit right there on Becky's kitchen table with the empty coffee mugs on that pretty lace tablecloth.

Now that I look back at that neat discussion, it wasn't all that bad, as time would eventually tell.

THE VISIT

The author, Ruth McCauley, and Becky Fonda
at the Fonda's kitchen table. (Bob McCauley)

PLANNING HENRY FONDA DAY

From the start, I hoped being together with the Fondas might help jump-start some idea or plan that could be put together by the Stuhr Museum to bring the Fonda family for a visit to Grand Island. Harriet Warren, Henry's sister in Omaha, and her daughter had visited and were very impressed with the Stuhr Museum and the little Fonda cottage. "Peter and Jane should come see it," she told me on the phone. The Stuhr Museum's director had voiced a great desire to do something that would get them here.

On the return home from our trip to Montana, I brought back no plan; only the feeling that the Fondas would be open to an idea if we could get it together. So with that, a committee was formed to make a plan. The second idea was to succeed for several reasons. The Stuhr Museum had an enthusiastic director in Sandi Yoder who had come to the Stuhr from Colonial Williamsburg. Also, Ted Turner had joined the Fonda family with his marriage to Jane. The Fondas all knew that we were putting forth a real effort to have a special Henry Fonda Day. Late in 1991, Ted told Jane, Peter, and Becky that, if the museum could get it together, he would see that the family could get there for it…on one condition: Jane's attendance would be kept top secret.

Every week, the committee met. The wheels began to turn slowly. We all threw out ideas to discuss. At times, it seemed we had almost come to a complete stop. At one point someone asked, "Ruth, do you think it's necessary to have this take place this year?" I emphatically said, "Yes!" A film festival of sorts was discussed over and over, and then we began cutting back to things we could handle. Suddenly ideas flowed. Since we could not bring Jane into the planning picture, most of the program began to settle around Peter. It was a tremendous undertaking, not only on the Stuhr's part, but for the Fonda family, also. The Friends of Henry Fonda was organized to help. Contacts were made with the Omaha Community Playhouse, which was most eager to help us in any way it could. The Stuhr Museum's exhibits designer and coordinator, Janelle Lindberg, immediately started an extensive research of Fonda memorabilia. Hollywood responded. Letters came from co-workers and friends like Jack Lemmon, Jimmy Stewart, and Dorothy McGuire. Harriet Warren, Jane Fonda, and Becky and Peter loaned some of Henry's paintings, leaving some of their walls quite noticeably bare. Douw Fonda loaned a bronze bust that he later gave to the Stuhr Museum. The Fondas were going to come and make it a family reunion. Yes sir, that Grand Island boy was going to have his day.

THIS PLACE IN ALL ITS SEASONS

JAMES STEWART

HENRY FONDA WAS MY BEST FRIEND. WE FIRST MET IN 1932, WHEN I WAS GETTING STARTED AS AN ACTOR IN NEW YORK CITY. HENRY HAD BEEN ACTING FOR SEVERAL YEARS.

ALTHOUGH 1932 WAS THE TIME OF THE COUNTRY'S WORST DEPRESSION, THE THEATRE BUSINESS IN NEW YORK HAD NEVER BEEN BETTER. HENRY AND I KEPT VERY BUSY. HE WAS IN THE PLAY "THE FARMER TAKES A WIFE" WHICH WAS BOUGHT FOR A MOVIE VERSION. HENRY WENT WITH IT TO HOLLYWOOD IN 1934.

IN 1935, I WAS SIGNED BY MGM AND ALSO WENT TO HOLLYWOOD WHERE HENRY AND I RENTED A HOUSE, AND NEVER STOPPED WORKING.

WHEN THE WAR CAME, HENRY WENT INTO THE NAVY, SERVING IN THE PACIFIC. WHEN THE WAR ENDED, HE WAS SIGNED FOR A PLAY ON BROADWAY, "MR. ROBERTS."

IT WAS A SMASH HIT. HENRY STAYED WITH THE PLAY THROUGH THE NEW YORK RUN AND ON THE ROAD AROUND THE COUNTRY. HE WAS IN THE PLAY MORE THAN TWO YEARS. HOLLYWOOD WAS HAPPY TO GET HIM BACK, AND OVER THE YEARS, HE STARRED IN MANY MORE MEMORABLE FILMS.

HENRY NEVER RETIRED. HE ALTERNATED FROM MOVIES TO PLAYS FROM YEAR TO YEAR. HE MADE A DISTINGUISHED CONTRIBUTION TO HIS PROFESSION. I AM HONORED TO PAY MY RESPECTS TO A GENTLEMAN AND A GREAT ACTOR - HENRY FONDA.

Jimmy Stewart

Letter from Jimmy Stewart

PLANNING HENRY FONDA DAY

As a true son of Nebraska, Henry fonda demonstrated to a world-wide audience a dedication to complete honesty in his work. Joshua Logan, the great director, described him as "Having within...an inextinguishable flame that burns in worship of the art of theatre"...he proved throughout his life that a boy, nurtured with values learned in Nebraska, understood the meaning of honor and lived accordingly.

—Gene Bunge and Marshal Jamison
Nebraska ETV Network

I never saw Hank Fonda play a scene in which he tried to bring attention to himself rather than carry out the author's intent. He would have considered such behavior a sacrilege. His respect for his craft was of the highest level, and his generosity when he was working with his fellow actors was enormous. Without any question, he must make every actor in the world proud to be a member of the same profession.

—Fellow actor, Jack Lemmon

HENRY FONDA DAY
A Fonda Family Reunion

On Saturday, August 15, 1992, the Fondas came to Grand Island. Besides Jane, Ted, and Peter and Becky, fifteen other Fonda family members would come by car to make this a tremendous family reunion. It was a joyous occasion. Harriet Warren from Omaha, and her daughter and husband from Colorado Springs, Colorado; Douw Fonda, Henry's favorite cousin, and his wife, Sue; their daughters and husbands and four little grandchildren arrived from Denver the night before so they would be able to meet the Turner jet as it arrived at the Grand Island airport the next morning. We introduced ourselves and made small talk as we waited with family members for the plane to appear in the northwest sky. It was fifteen minutes late, then it touched down and taxied closer and closer. When the engines shut down, screaming delighted children ran to welcome them. Everyone hugged and kissed. As John Springer said: "The Fondas could not be closer as a family."

The *Grand Island Independent* headlines read: "Grand Island Shares Fonda Reunion." The *Omaha World-Herald* responded with kindly editorials. The first stop on the fast-paced tour headed by the Grand Island Police Department, was St. Stephen's Episcopal Church to have a look at the baptismal records of Henry Jaynes Fonda, who was christened there on Dec. 26, 1905. This was an especially poignant moment for the family, Douw making special note that his parents had been there as witnesses. They probably came by train from Omaha for Christmas and the next day attended Henry's christening. "I never knew that," Douw said. It seemed a very pleasant way to start out this special day.

The entourage proceeded to the 622 address on West Division Street, where the Henry Fonda birth house originally stood prior to its relocation to the Railroad Town of the Stuhr Museum. Our car with Peter and Becky made a short detour to McDonald's to pick up a hamburger for Peter who was conducting a workshop on "The Art of Filmmaking" at the Walnut Junior High School, where "down in front near the stage a flock of Fonda relatives took their seats all reassuring to see them rub shoulders with local folk," the *Omaha World-Herald* reported.

At St. Stephen's Episcopal Church, the family viewing Henry's baptismal record. From front, Harriet Warren, Peter and Jane Fonda. (Stuhr Archives)

PETER FONDA'S WORKSHOP

After introductions, Peter Fonda, relaxed in jeans and an open-necked shirt, seemed to relish his time on stage at Walnut Junior High School with the students, guests, and members of his family in the audience, to whom he often referred to Henry as "our father, her brother, her uncle, and their cousin." Peter, the professional, has the knack of making the audience feel a part of the program. Besides being an award-winning actor, producer, director, and writer, Peter Fonda is a very good speaker and excellent teacher.

"I was eighteen when I played Elwood Dowd, a seventy-two-year-old character in *Harvey* at the Omaha Community Playhouse. I didn't know it, but my dad was in the audience and he paid me the compliment of saying I didn't overact the old age aspect, as many young actors do." In discussing his experience in his award-winning movie, *Easy Rider*, his father was not so complimentary. When the film was released, his father felt unsure and scared for him after seeing the film. "He didn't think it would fly." Even Jane was worried about Peter's effort. "She said to me after the screening, 'I don't get it.'" But the film ended by winning the Best First Work of the 1979 Cannes Film Festival.

PETER FONDA'S WORKSHOP

After an hour of speaking about film-making and fielding questions, Peter's Aunt Harriet [Fonda Warren], who Peter stayed with in Omaha while attending the University of Omaha, came up to her nephew "just to give him a kiss."

LUNCHEON
Henry Fonda Day

*A*t the luncheon following the workshop at the Midtown Holiday Inn, the Omaha Community Playhouse participated by providing a reading from a Playhouse production in which Henry had appeared, along with songs from their upcoming production of *The Whiz*. Peter and Jane presented the prestigious Henry Fonda Memorial Scholarships to two graduating high schools seniors. "This is a very moving event and it makes us all proud to be here," Jane said. "Both of these young people have already accomplished so much and we wish them continued success. I know if Dad were here, he'd say, 'Wow!'" Peter quipped, "These are very lovely. I wish I had one of these."

Our local organization, the Friends of Henry Fonda, presented Peter and Becky, Jane and her husband Ted Turner, and their Aunt Harriet each with hand-crafted kaleidoscopes by the well-known Nebraska artist, Ralph Olson. At this time, all Grand Islanders had an opportunity to meet and visit with the Fondas, and vice versa.

HENRY FONDA MEMORIAL HIGHWAY

Next stop and down the road apiece, they were holding up traffic just outside the gate of the museum entrance where a special dedication of the Henry Fonda Memorial Highway, a 5.6-mile stretch of Highway 34 and 281 to the Hamilton County line, was taking place. Jane thanked the State of Nebraska, calling the dedication "a great honor to the Fonda family," and thanked the museum for putting Henry Fonda Day together and for preserving her father's birthplace home. Peter also gave his thanks and joked he'd like to see his name on the sign, too. "I'd planned to wait until the crowd cleared, then have my picture taken holding up a sign in front of this one, so it would say, "Peter Henry Fonda Memorial Highway." He also remarked, "When I was going to college, this would have made a great drag strip."

When it was time to unveil the sign, Jane and Peter invited the entire family to participate in removing the green covering which didn't seem to want to come off—it took a lot of tugging. When it finally did, the crowd cheered, the family smiled and clapped and hugged each other. Then, the cars that had been held up came honking and whizzing by.

The family at the dedication of the Henry Fonda Memorial Highway. At left with cane is Douw Fonda, Henry's favorite cousin and a close, lifelong friend. (Stuhr Archives)

A VISIT TO THE BIRTHPLACE

They came; sixteen of them. Their daughter Harriet, their grandchildren, Jane and Peter, nephew Douw, with their respective wives, husbands, children, and grandchildren—all descendants and relatives of William and Herberta Fonda—came for a visit eighty-seven years after they had lived there. The family Fonda, four generations, came to see where "their father, their brother, their uncle, their cousin" had been born. It was the first time for most. Harriet had visited a few years earlier. I had the pleasure of joining them inside the house to watch their reactions. Through the years, I had sent pictures to Jane, Peter and Becky, and also Harriet and Douw and Sue, but Becky looked at me and said, "It just looks so lived in." Then I knew she had gotten it. An added surprise was when someone turned the voice recorder on and there was Henry himself saying, "Welcome to the Fonda house," and telling about the house and his connection to it. Ted Turner even played a tune on the old piano. They spent about an hour enjoying the house, iced tea, lemonade, and ginger molasses cookies under the shade tree in the front yard. Here, my husband caught a sweet picture of Jane, sitting on Ted's lap enjoying the visit with her Aunt Harriet.

Yes, the press was there to record, but they were very careful not to take away from the moment. A family group picture was taken on the front porch and another one of Harriet, Peter, and Jane was taken in the bedroom where Henry was born. "This is the first time we've been here," Jane said, following the tour. "It's wonderful to come here and see Dad's house. It's moving and special." Peter added, "I now have a sense of what it was like when he lived here in Grand Island." The whole Stuhr Museum concept and Railroad Town impressed Peter.

The family gathers on the porch of the Fonda cottage. (Bob McCauley)

A VISIT TO THE BIRTHPLACE

Jane Fonda, her husband Ted Turner, and Henry's sister Harriet Warren at tea on Henry Fonda Day. (Bob McCauley)

Peter and Jane Fonda and Harriet Warren in the bedroom of the Fonda cottage. (Stuhr Museum)

DINNER

That evening, the family returned for a reception and dinner in their honor in the main gallery of the museum where an exhibit highlighted the life of Henry Fonda who never forgot his Nebraska roots. Janelle Lindberg, the museum exhibits coordinator, had gathered over sixty items from New York City to Hollywood. The exhibit was made possible with the cooperation of Fonda family members and friends, Fonda Productions, the Academy of Motion Picture Arts and Sciences, the Omaha Community Playhouse, and Western Costume Company of North Hollywood, Ron Hull of Nebraska Education Television, and other sources. There were letters of tribute from entertainers and friends like Jimmy Stewart, Dorothy McGuire, Jack Lemmon, and Eddie Albert, plus a very special showing of Fonda's paintings. My favorite of the whole exhibit was his painting of three battered hats that he had done while filming *On Golden Pond*. The story goes that, when he began work with Katharine Hepburn on the film, Miss Hepburn brought him an old hat to wear that had been worn by Spencer Tracy, one of her other co-stars. It became one of three hats Fonda wore in the filming. Knowing of his artistry, Miss Hepburn asked Fonda for one of his paintings. He created the one of the three old hats in the exhibit and gave it to her.

After the dinner, historian Dr. Robert Manley provided an entertaining perspective of Grand Island in 1905—the year Henry Fonda was born. Peter reminisced about his father flying kites, but before he began to tell the story, he noted that my "Aunt Harriet, Ruth McCauley, and wife Becky, have worked a long time to get this together."

That is when that cup I left sitting on the table with the lace tablecloth in Becky's Montana kitchen on our visit three years before was refilled, and "my cup runneth over" with the joy I felt on this whole day of events. It was a great day for Grand Island, Nebraska.

The photo above was taken of Henry Fonda at the Omaha Community Playhouse Theater while he acknowledges a standing ovation honoring his half-century of accomplishments on stage, screen, and television. As he wiped tears from his eyes, he said, "Fondas are known to cry over a good steak." He went on to discuss his beginnings at the Omaha Community Playhouse and to answer audience questions for some 45 minutes. (Omaha Community Playhouse)

MAY 16, 1905
A Reminiscence by Dr. Robert Manley

*I*f you look at the *Grand Island Independent* and come across the issue of May 13, 1904, you'll find this small insert: "W.B. Fonda has decided to go to housekeeping and accordingly he has procured a residence on West Division Street where he and his family will be at home to their friends."

Now I have a feeling that one of the reputable real estate groups in Grand Island was involved in that transaction because Gil and Houston were developing that part of Grand Island. And the Gil and Houston ad in that paper said you could buy a five-room house on West Division Street for $1,500.

I think probably William Fonda undoubtedly had many friends and many acquaintances. Salesmen usually do. And among his product line was one carried by the National Biscuit Company. Now you have to follow this pretty closely because this is also my concluding line.

One of his products was Uneeda Biscuit. "For the woman whose work is never done, Uneeda Biscuit. The crackle you hear is the sign they are fresh. Uneeda Biscuits for 5 cents."

Well, William and Herberta Fonda had come to Grand Island from Omaha. And that was not an uncommon arrangement. One of the curious phenomenons of the Platte Valley is the connection of Grand Island with Omaha.

The first store along the trail here, Konig Store, the OK Store that all of you Grand Islanders know about, was actually named from Mr. Konig's brother's store in Omaha, the OK Store in Omaha

George Thummel, who for years was the leading attorney in this community, was from Omaha and lived here a number of years and then went back.

And C.F. Bentley, a young man from Freeport who wanted to go into the banking business, stopped in Omaha to visit with the Millard brothers and ask them where a young man might open a bank, and the Millard brothers recommended that Mr. Bentley come to Grand Island, where he started the Grand Island Banking House and later worked with Sam Wolbach, who established the First National Bank.

So, in short, the National Biscuit Company sent William and whoever was his employer to a very prosperous territory. And, as a salesman, he had railroads going in all directions. We had five railroads coming into Grand Island with about 40 trains every day.

By early 1900, the hard times of the 1890s were a dim recollection. Prosperity was here, seemingly permanently. The Grand Island Sugar Company was leading the United States in production of sugar. The year 1904, we turned out 1.5 million pounds of sugar and the German farmers around here who were raising beets were getting $5 a ton and happy with it.

And since the town was prosperous, the educators were down and called on the Chamber of Commerce, yes sir. In fact, the president of the Grand Island Baptist College called on the Chamber to point out how important to the economic development of Grand Island that college was and

MAY 16, 1905

how the businessmen should support Grand Island Baptist College.

Also, we were still a pioneer town because in that year Fred Heady and Lowen Stolle, members of the first colony that came here from Davenport, Iowa, were still walking the streets of Grand Island.

One of the big events in Nebraska was the GAI encampment which occurred in Grand Island shortly before Henry was born. These boys were the old Union veterans, the men who had served in the Civil War. And we had the Soldiers Home here and that meant that every year thousands of these veterans came to Grand Island. We were a convention center.

Now unfortunately, as time passed, the numbers of men dwindled from thousands into hundreds. But in 1904 and 1905, we had our last great land rush. The Grand Island newspapers are filled with notices of young men and young women who are leaving Grand Island and heading for the Sandhills to take a Kinkaid homestead, the last land rush in this country.

Gadstreet and Fletcher had the largest horse and mule market in the United States and it was here in Grand Island. And I don't know where they got the critters, but the day they advertised this huge auction was the day a group of farmers south of town set up their goods at Chicago prices. And Max Hager the jeweler announced that he now had the Kodak camera, that was going to revolutionize that industry, for sale.

Wolbach Department Store offered clothing for men and women both. It offered to the women fashionable shirtwaists at $1 to $2.50 apiece, and spring tailored suits for $2.95. And they said these came direct from the markets in New York City and, friends, you could trust the Wolbachs absolutely. They spoke the truth indeed.

THIS PLACE IN ALL ITS SEASONS

At the Rosier's Beehive Grocery, bread was 5 cents, sugar was 17 pounds for $1, eggs 23 cents a dozen, tea one pound for 25 cents, a can of pork and beans 10 cents, a three-pound can of peaches 15 cents, sardines 5 cents a tin.

For entertainment, you went to the Bartenbach Opera House. If you were in for a wonderful evening of highbrow entertainment, there was opera very often. But more often, Mr. Bartenbach complained about the fact that nobody attended the opera, but they did show up for the vaudeville shows.

Folks were talking in town. There were lots of things to talk about. The big argument was prohibition. Is Grand Island going to close down the saloons? Well, you know what the answer to that one was.

The second question was, what about municipal ownership of our electric light plant?

And down at Hart's Gun Store, Mr. Hart announced that he was bringing in a Rambler automobile for people to look at. And yet in the newspaper, it was pointed out that don't think that that automobile is a thing of the future because everybody knows that that engine pollutes the environment so badly that Tom Edison is working on a battery in his laboratory back in New Jersey and the horseless carriage is going to be electrically powered. Don't pay any attention to those gasoline engines.

And in a tight mayor's race, Henry Schuff, who was the genial manager of the Vienna Restaurant, was elected mayor. His opponent said he's nothing but a pie shuffler. But Henry showed them he had the ability and his reign as mayor was one of prosperity.

Our high school had a graduation uncommon in the number of kids that graduated. We had 21 kids graduate from high school; 9 girls and 12 boys. And that was uncommon.

MAY 16, 1905

But the big news was that Teddy Roosevelt himself, the man who epitomized and represented the optimism and enthusiasm of America in 1905, was coming again to Grand Island. He had been here in 1903, and now he was coming back, and while he was here, he was going to dedicate the new library.

And the newspaper noted that two days before the president arrived, secret service agents were setting up his visit and where he could appear. And it was a somber note in the newspaper that said never forget that, in our generation, we have seen three presidents assassinated. And so there were extra precautions taken as President Teddy Roosevelt came into Grand Island.

Well, if you looked at the *Independent*, there was important news going on in the world. I don't know how many folks in Grand Island actually grasped how important the events were that were unfolding in the world.

Particularly over in the Far East, where the Russians and the Japanese were at war, and the Japanese and the Russian fleet were going to meet early in 1905 at the battle of Kershamon. And the Japanese squadron was going to be totally destroyed in one of the most decisive and bloody horrendous battles ever fought on the high seas.

But what emerged from that was Japan as a major world power. While Teddy was here in Grand Island, he noted to one of the reporters that it was up to him as president of the United States to bring peace between the Japanese and the Russians, and to preserve Russia as a power. It did appear to him, he said, that two things were clear: One, that one day the United States will go to war with Japan. And number two, that Russia was fast disintegrating. Because as Russia faced these military defeats, the people at home went into the streets to riot. And there was a hopeful headline in the *Grand Island Independent* that said "Russia Is on the Road to Democracy."

THIS PLACE IN ALL ITS SEASONS

And that was in 1905.

People could see these things in the world and in the nation, but I have a feeling that in that generation people are just as they are today. The important thing going on in the Fonda household was that there was a baby on the way.

And chances are that the call went to Dr. Roeder. Dr. Roeder's advertisement in the newspaper was most impressive. He was a surgeon at St. Francis Hospital, which meant he operated on a lot of poor people who could not pay because you know that only poor people went to the hospital in those days.

But he also was the consulting surgeon for the Union Pacific Railroad. And he was an examining surgeon for all of the old veterans. A man of real competence.

His office was at 115 West Third Street. His telephone number was 299, and I have a feeling William called him and Dr. Roeder made a house call. And he came to that little house on West Division Street.

And on May 17, 1905, the *Independent* carried this short notice:

> Dr. Roeder reports Uneeda Biscuits for sale at any old price from salesman William Brace Fonda this morning, a bright baby boy having arrived at the home of Mr. and Mrs. Fonda on West Division Street yesterday afternoon. Both mother and little one are getting along nicely.

That was May 16, 1905. And on that very day, one of the Grand Island High School graduates, whose name was listed in the paper, was Grant Reynolds, who was going to become one of the great artists in the first half of the 20th Century.

And in that same paper, hired to teach in the Grand Island public schools was Grace Abbott, who was going to live her life as one of the great women in American history.

MAY 16, 1905

And one of the young men who came back to visit in Grand Island on this very date was Arthur Bentley, the son of the banker and graduate of John Hopkins University who is today recognized as one of the five most important intellectual figures in the 20th Century.

An artist, a health care provider, and a woman's advocate. Grace, of course, was the first woman to hold a real high position in our federal government

And at the Bartenbach Opera House, hear this:

"Come tonight and see the greatest moving picture exhibition ever given here at the Opera House. It is the future."

And at that house on West Division Street, there was a baby boy—Henry Fonda. May 16, 1905—an exciting day.

FLYING KITES WITH HENRY
By Peter Fonda

My Aunt Harriet sent me something from a newspaper; an article from a magazine written many years ago about different folks and who their heroes were. One of the articles was about my father, and he said that his hero was his father. Now I had never known this, and my father never said much about his life to us. I did know that he enjoyed flying kites. This article did tell me that he remembered his father taking him out to fly kites on Sunday. His interest in kites began with his father, William Brace Fonda.

After my father's death, his dear friend Jimmy Stewart arrived at his house. Jimmy sat there quietly for quite some time. He finally said, "You know, I remember the kites." And then there was a long pause until the rest of the kite stories came out.

Jimmy was right. He and my father flew kites. I tried to learn about my father by listening to the conversations he would have with Stewart. He was like a godfather to me. The conversations were very simple.

"Ah, Hank?"

"Yeah."

"Where does this piece go?"

"Well, let's see. That goes over on A-23."

"O.K. Yup."

That was it. To B-23, C-23, slot A to B & C. Then there was the laying of the cover on this magnificent glider with an eight-foot wingspan. This was all being done for me. Right? Fat chance. I was six years old and this thing was bigger than I was and weighed more than me. But I was amazed by it all. I was amazed by the patience my father had in putting those little pieces of balsawood together and putting paper on top of it. I was amazed by the amount of conversation that was not held between him and his best friend.

Well, the glider was built and the day came to fly it. Father had put together a marlin fishing reel to hold the line and it was cut off at the first little doohickey that the line goes through. He had a leather thing that would let the line feed out to this enormous kite that would go way up in the air. And then he showed me how to send the kite messages. I don't know how many of you have ever flown a kite before, but those who have not sent a message to the pilot are missing a grand piece of kite flying. You take something like a matchbook cover and rip it a bit and put it around the line and it would go up like a whirligig; up the line drawn by the wind and that was a message to the pilot.

My father gave me this rig to hold. I remember how much it weighed. I grabbed onto the rod and I was scooting across the ground. *Swoosh!* With father running, thank God. After I saw *Drums Along the Mohawk*, I knew why my father ran so fast. He was able to grab me before I got through the trees, across the canyon, and over to my grandmother's house.

This glider was taken out many times and I would go out and watch my father. He would run with these long strides with the glider in hand and he would let it go and stop and watch it. Then he would pick it up again and put the wings back on properly. I would take some clay out of its nose or I would put more clay back in its nose. Proper balance. My father was a perfectionist. There were many days of running and just letting this thing go and watching whether it would turn right or left, down or up, and adding or taking away a little bit of clay each time. It would fly almost to the property line and gently glide down. He was satisfied.

I don't know how he did it, ingeniously of course; he rigged it so that when it got to the top of the line on its hook, he could shake it and the glider cut loose. At first it just drifted off. I was going, "Oh, no." I knew what happened when it didn't go and it crashed and they would have to build a new wing. It soon took wing and got its aerodynamics and began circling a little bit and then began to head west. We got in our old Ford woody and drove up our road and past grandmother's house. We were trying to chase this glider and I was more and more worried as the glider got further away from us.

I couldn't quite discover what was in my father's mind. There was a very funny look in his face and I will never forget it. It just kept flying. He finally stopped trying to chase it. And I realized he really wasn't trying to chase it. He was watching it. For him it was the perfect thing. This humongous piece of paper and balsa that had taken him months with Jimmy Stewart to build had gone on its own toward the sun. Just continually flying up to the Santa Monica mountains. He was pleased as punch. He never wanted to see it again. It took me a long time to figure that out.

Peter Fonda told this story at the dinner held at the Fonda family reunion at Stuhr Museum on August 15, 1992.

SUNDAY BREAKFAST

While Jane and Ted left soon after dinner the night before for their ranch in New Mexico, the rest of the family stayed overnight to spend more time together and see more of the Stuhr Museum of the Prairie Pioneer where an outdoor breakfast was served them at their "father's, brother's, uncle's and cousin's house." Karen Anderson had participated in all of the events of Fonda Day, introducing Peter at the workshop and later at lunch. As president of Friends of Henry Fonda, she presented kaleidoscopes to family members and, later that afternoon, she and friend Carol Congrove served tea under the shade tree in the garden while the family leisurely wandered in and out of the house.

The next morning, Karen was up at 4 A.M. to start preparing breakfast for this famous family, calling on memories of her own grandmother's recipes for ideas. The long tables, brought out by museum staff, were covered with blue and white checkered tablecloths. Centerpieces were Ball canning jars filled with brown-eyed Susans and homemade jellies, jams, and butter, stretched out on each table. Karen's sister and friend Carol were dressed in 1905 era fashions to add to the occasion. A wicker baby buggy was pushed out on the lawn in memory of the baby Henry and was used as a prop for family pictures. The food was prepared and kept warm on the old-fashioned black range and taken hot from the oven to the buffet table as soon as the guests arrived.

Just like Henry's memories of his family going on picnics in their automobile over dirt roads, this morning started with the entire family being picked up in different vintage automobiles and ushered in via the back dirt road, past the old steepled Danish Lutheran Church and the little red school house, and on down the road where they pulled up to the iron gate of the Fonda yard. Here they disembarked and joined us waiting to greet them, including Roger Welsch and his wife, Linda. Roger is a humorist, Nebraska folklorist, and writer, who is a regular on *CBS Sunday Morning* with his "Postcards from Nebraska" segment. Bob and I, and friend Lois Jones who had come for the entire event from Estes Park, Colorado, served as hosts. After breakfast and hugs and praises for the cook, the family spread out over Railroad Town, meeting locals and taking carriage rides and taking pictures for their own family albums. They all conceded that it was the best time of all.

SUNDAY BREAKFAST

Outside the Fonda cottage.

Back row: Linda and Roger Welsch, Peter Fonda; Front row: Ruth McCauley, Becky Fonda.
(Bob McCauley)

Wicker baby buggy and summer flowers at Fonda cottage.

BESSIE'S SUGAR COOKIES

*A*s I sat in the yard of the Fonda cottage enjoying this country breakfast with members of the Fonda family, Douw Fonda, Henry's cousin, told the story of "Bessie's Sugar Cookies." When Douw was only eight years old, his mother, Ethelyn Hinners Fonda, died. His father, Ten Eyck Fonda, Jr., hired a housekeeper named Bessie Vicorine. Bessie took loving care of Douw, his two brothers Hilton and Garett, and his sister Virginia. Douw fondly remembered "what a wonderful cook she was. At holiday times, the house always smelled of marvelous cakes, pies, and all kinds of cookies baking in the oven." Douw's cousins Henry, Harriet, and Jayne were there often to help sample whatever Bessie was baking. One of Henry's favorites was a crisp, orange flavored sugar cookie that she made. When the children grew up, Bessie remained as housekeeper for twenty-seven years.

One year, during the Christmas holidays, when Henry was appearing in a play at a Chicago theatre, Bessie baked a batch of Henry's favorite sugar cookies, packed them neatly in a box, and tied the box with a big red ribbon. She caught a ride to Chicago with a truck driver friend and delivered then in person to a surprised Henry Fonda. She was treated royally with a front row seat and was invited backstage after the performance. Henry passed the cookies around to cast and crew. Everyone wanted the recipe. After that first bite. Bessie's sugar cookies were expected at Christmas wherever Henry was.

Ever since Douw and Sue Fonda were married, Bessie's sugar cookies have been an important tradition in their home. Sue makes dozens of the paper-thin cookies and explicitly follows the directions Bessie gave her. Sue has already made sure that daughters, Pat, Tina, and Page know how to make these cookies.

My thanks to Douw Fonda for sharing this lovely family story and to Sue who has given us Bessie's famous recipe.

Bessie's Sugar Cookies

Makes "a zillion," depending on how thin you roll them, the size, the shape, and how close you place the cutters. Don't let the dough dry out.

The excellence of this rolled, slightly orange flavored sugar cookie depends on how thin it is rolled. I was instructed to firmly clip a pastry cloth onto a counter (Bessie used a marble slab), use a pastry cloth cover on a rolling pin, both floured slightly, and keep renewing the "dusting" of both the cloth and the pin as you roll out each batch. Bessie always said, "the secret is you roll it until you can read a newspaper through it." I say, "Maybe almost."

THIS PLACE IN ALL ITS SEASONS

Ingredients

½ cup butter or shortening
1 egg
5 tsps. baking powder
Rind of one orange, grated

1 cup sugar
2 3/4 cups unsifted flour
5 Tbs. orange juice

Combine, chill in refrigerator, cover.

You can freeze dough at this point. Wrap the dough in foil in one or more balls. After the batches thaw, you may need to use more flour on the board before rolling out.

Use small amounts of dough to roll out and keep the rest of the dough covered in the refrigerator in case you are interrupted. Be stingy-place the cutters close together. It is best to only roll out once.

Sprinkle with white or colored granulated sugar, decorettes, or chopped almonds. Press the décor lightly into each cookie to make it stick. Bake in 375° oven for 7 to 10 minutes on greased cookie sheets. WATCH! Time may vary, so go on the low side to be safe. Bake until lightly brown. Remove at once. Cool. Store in tins—out of reach!

Variations: The Fondas always had some wreaths cut with a doughnut cutter trimmed with red hots or bits of cherries. You can use colored icings to paint angels, Santas, trees, reindeer, etc., and make the cookie a bit thicker. Food coloring added to granulated sugar and mixed well works in a shaker with large holes. It is cheap and fun to get different shades of color. Save your old spice containers for this.

—Contribution from Sue Fonda

THE HENRY FONDA ROSE GARDEN
Read at Dedication

The idea of the Henry Fonda Rose was planted back in 1987 in the office of Warren Rodgers. Together, we were discussing the possibility of a Henry Fonda Rose. Neither of us knew how to go about it, but Warren took the initiative to contact the American Rose Society. They answered saying that, for a rose to be accepted by their society usually took a number of years and the cost would run from $5,000 to $25,000. Needless to say, the rose stopped there temporarily.

When the Friends of Henry Fonda was organized, one of our long-term goals was to somehow find a way to have a Henry Fonda Rose created. On Henry Fonda Day and the day of the Fonda family reunion in 1992, Karen Anderson, our president, mentioned this at the luncheon program. Betty Kinzie enthusiastically pursued information from different sources.

Soon afterward, an article appeared in *Modern Maturity* magazine about a fellow in California who developed and helped patent several roses which brought him added income. There was an address for a kit with directions. So our group voted to spend $25 for the kit and we put it in the capable hands of Carol Congrove who loves to grow roses.

In the meantime, Carol had an opportunity to talk with Nancy Butler of Jackson & Perkins growers. They were hybridizing new roses all the time, so I followed up with a phone call to Nancy and told her what we had in mind. She repeated, in effect, what she had told Carol. 1) They first would need the permission of the Fonda family to name a rose after Henry. 2) They wanted to know the special color and type of rose preferred by the Fonda family. 3) It would take two or more years to get the right rose. 4) No; this would not cost us a thing. Nancy was pleased we had asked, and they were definitely interested. They had created many well-known roses, including their recent Lucille Ball Rose.

Becky Fonda was well aware of what we were attempting to get done. When I called her, she was ecstatic. "Oh the family will be thrilled!" When we discussed the color, our thinking was a bright golden yellow to remind everyone of Henry's award winning film, *On Golden Pond*. I did not know until sometime later that Peter and Jane agreed. They also decided on Henry's favorite—a tea rose. We were in business!

Nancy Butler was in touch with the Fondas throughout 1993, and also kept me informed of the progress. I passed all information on to the Friends of Henry Fonda and Warren Rodgers at the Stuhr Museum.

I knew a special rose was being considered in the fall of 1993. I called Becky Fonda to see if it had arrived and Peter answered the phone. As soon as he heard my voice he exclaimed, "Oh, Ruth, we have the Henry Fonda Rose! It's magnificent! The scent! The color! All just perfect!" I cannot explain my feelings; only that it was like the birth of a special child.

In February of 1994, I received the transparency of the rose, and Bob and I had it developed. This was our first look!

Soon after, a call came from Nancy Butler. They were preparing sneak preview fliers of the Henry Fonda Rose and needed an informal, face forward view of Henry. So far, the Fondas had not been able to come up with just what they wanted. Did I have any suggestions? I mentioned the American Film Institute and then remembered that *House Beautiful* magazine had devoted an entire issue to the Fonda home and lifestyle when they lived on Tigertail Road in Bel Aire. I suggested she contact the archives of the magazine. I believe it was there she found the picture that was used. The *House Beautiful* story had a special section devoted to "farmer Fonda" and the article told how Henry had appeared on a Ford radio program. He was told he could receive his pay either in cash or merchandise; his choice of a Ford, Mercury, or Lincoln. He thought for a moment of his land, his garden, and of the hauling he had to do and, turning to the man, he said, "I'd like a tractor."

At the groundbreaking of the Stuhr Museum, Bob and I met the famous architect Edward Durrell Stone. We took a special part in the 1991 Henry Fonda Day tribute and Fonda family reunion, and in May, I participated in the dedication of the Henry Fonda Rose Garden. I am so lucky! As Henry Fonda was proud of his paying for moving the Fonda cottage to the Stuhr grounds, I also feel great pride having walked step by step, with others, through the process of this special rose and making of the garden. I was even honored to select the gift given the garden by the Fondas. A sculpture was considered, but Peter said, "The garden is the sculpture, Ruth. Henry did not like nature infringed upon." So a simple 9x5 bronze plaque was selected and inscribed with the words:

HENRY FONDA ROSE GARDEN DEDICATED MAY 14, 1995

The plaque will be placed on the column that graces the center of the "wheel" walk that defines the garden.

THIS PLACE IN ALL ITS SEASONS

No one could have been more professional and easy to work with than Nancy Butler of Jackson & Perkins. She listened to every suggestion and wish. There was little nudging on my part on behalf of family wishes. Jackson & Perkins not only developed the rose which has been registered with the American Rose Society, but they also generously donated the needed plants, funds, and the design expertise to create this garden. Warren Rodgers took it from there.

Ribbon cutting at the Fonda Rose Garden.
(Ken Bolten)

THE HENRY FONDA ROSE GARDEN

Henry Fonda Memorial Rose Garden

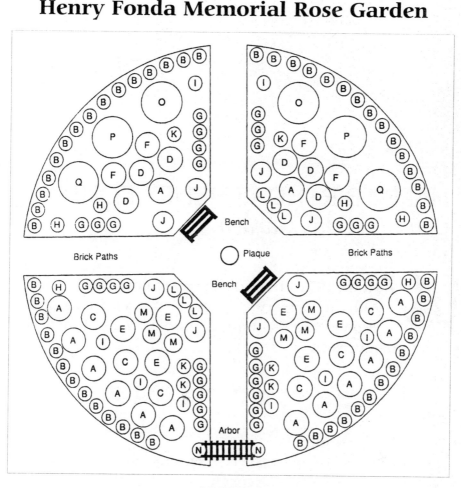

LEGEND

ROSES:
A   14–Henry Fonda (HF)
     (Yellow, a favorite of Mr. Fonda)
B   56–Lady of the Dawn
C   6–French Lace (FL)
D   6–Legend (LEG)
E   6–Love Potion (LP)
F   4–Sheer Bliss (SB)

PERENNIALS:
G   32–Munstead Lavender
H   6–White Delphinium
I   8–Blue Delphinium

J   8–Peony "Raspberry Sundae"
     (a favorite of Mr. Fonda)
K   6–Achillea "Red Beauty"
L   6–Shasta Daisy "Little Princess"
M   6–Daylily "Catherine Woodbury"
N   2–Clematis "Nelly Moser"

LILACS:
O   2 each of 'Madame Lemoine'
P   "Belle de Nancy"
Q   "Alphonse Lavalle"

DESIGNED BY:
Michael Cady, JACKSON & PERKINS

HAPPY BIRTHDAY HENRY FONDA
God Bless this Garden

With the dedication of the Fonda Rose Garden on the 90th anniversary of Henry Fonda's birth came correspondence from many people close to him and to the garden project.

From Peter Fonda:

"Henry Fonda was very serious about making his beautiful gardens grow. Henry liked to think of himself as a simple man, a midwestern farmer. One of our father's favorite writers was Henry David Thoreau. Here is our father's idea of a reading, short and to the point."

> A single gentle rain makes the grass many shades greener. So our prospects brighten on the influx of better thoughts. We should be blessed if we lived in the present always, and took advantage of every accident that befell us, like the grass which confesses the influence of

the slightest dew that falls on it; and did not spend our time in atoning for the neglect of past opportunities, which we call doing our duty. We loiter in winter while it is already spring. In a pleasant spring morning all men's sins are forgiven. As every season seems best to us in its turn, so the coming in of spring is like the creation of cosmos out of chaos and the realization of the Golden Age.

From Harriet Warren [Henry's sister]:

It is always lovely to hear that Henry's friends at the Stuhr are again honoring him; this time on the occasion of his 90th birthday on May 16.

Thank you for all your wonderful efforts.

From Douw and Sue Fonda [Henry's cousin and his wife]:

Our—your—Henry's—yellow rose is happily planted and doing well in Denver. This beautiful commemorative rose...will keep us connected to Grand Island and all the Friends of Henry Fonda and the Stuhr Museum. How amazed and pleased Hank would be to see a yellow rose bush with his name on it! It is indeed a special addition to our garden, as well as the gardens of the rest of the Fonda family from California to Arizona to Colorado to Montana and Nebraska.

We secured another rose bush from Jackson & Perkins and have donated it to the Denver Botanic Gardens. It will be in the garden there by the front door for all to enjoy. We toured these gardens with Henry and Shirlee several times.

I'm sure he would be proud of this addition to our Denver gardens. And to think of another whole garden as a birthday present at the Stuhr Museum location is the icing on the cake!

From Dorothy McGuire:
What joy to look at roses and feel the spirit of Henry Fonda.

From Martha Forrest, Vice President of Marketing, Jackson & Perkins:
Jackson & Perkins is happy to join with you in recognizing, Mr. Fonda's 90th birthday through this dedication of the Henry Fonda Rose Garden at the Stuhr Museum of the Prairie Pioneer. It is our hope that this garden will be a symbol to all who visit the museum of the affable and dynamic spirit of one of America's great performers.

THE HENRY FONDA ROSE
By Ken Bolton

With sturdy roots in midwest soil
Both to nurture and to grow
And survive life on the prairie
In the *wind*, the *rain*, the *snow*
Then to take with you, this hardiness
A tremendous journey...it may seem
From the most meager of beginnings
Toward a yet unfinished dream
With offspring, following your footsteps
Each in their own way...given room
Offered a gentle hand and kindness
To *live* their lives, to *grow*, to *bloom*
In commemoration of your birthday
We begin a life...anew
Through the use of *spades* and *shovels* and *love*
And, "With A Fonda Cottage View"
You've earned a world's respect and honor
Now your *Friends*...gather and propose
To return back to your garden
The Henry Fonda Rose.

DEEP ROOTS DO FONDAS GROW

*E*ven though Peter and Jane grew up in their father's limelight, the lyrics, "Father may have and Mother may have, but God bless the child who has his own" stands. Henry had taken care of the expenses for having the house of his birth moved to the Stuhr Museum grounds, had given money for its restoration, and visited a time or two to see the finished results. But after the initial work was done, he evidently never thought about its future upkeep. After his death and his will was read, there was no allowance given for the upkeep of his home. In fact, I am sure he never even considered it, thinking he had done all that was necessary and the rest would be taken care of by the Hall County residents. With a letter from Jack Learned, then the museum's director, we wrote to Peter, Jane, and Shirlee. The family had a conference of sorts, and the outcome was a generous sum donated to the Stuhr Museum Foundation for the birthplace's perpetual maintenance.

Although Peter and Jane live incredibly busy lives elsewhere, they do come back to Nebraska, such as for Henry Fonda Day in 1992. Peter participated in the Great Plains Film Festival in 1997 in Lincoln. And...in 1998, Peter and

Becky lent their names to the Stuhr 2000 financial campaign.

Becky always sees that the entire family signs a Christmas card during their Thanksgiving vacation that is mailed to arrive for our old-fashioned Christmas at the house, and there is a standing order at a local florist for a centerpiece for the dining room table to be delivered from the family for the Henry Fonda birthday celebration. Jane Fonda and Ted Turner have purchased ranch land in northwestern Nebraska where they raise buffalo. The closest little town is Mullin, with a population of 320 people. Recently, they gave a $25,000 gift to the little village to help generate activities for the young people in the vicinity. It will certainly make a difference in their lives.

Although Henry and his beloved sister Harriet are gone, the Fonda legacy continues through the family of Henry Fonda.

"I LOVE OMAHA"

While Peter Fonda was attending school in Omaha and staying with his Aunt Harriet and Uncle Jack Peacock, he wrote a letter to the Public Pulse column of the *Omaha World-Herald*.

"I love Omaha," he wrote. "I buy my clothes here and people go to the theater for the right reason. Because they love it and not just to be seen there." When I read that in my morning paper, I was impressed. How special that the son of Henry Fonda would take time and put pen to paper and tell the readers of that column that he loved Omaha. I felt he must be a very sensitive young man who could see beneath the beauty of Omaha. I later was to learn that Peter Fonda loves the Sandhills of Nebraska, as well. I related to his writing, for at that same time I was writing a series of articles similar to Steinbeck's *Travels With Charlie* for the *Omaha World-Herald Sunday Magazine of the Midlands*.

I went to great lengths to write about what to see and do in Omaha, and Peter stated it so well in three words: "I love Omaha."

It is amazing to me how many people don't see Nebraska for its beauty as they fly over or drive through from here to there on Interstate 80. This is true not only for those who travel through it, but also for people who call themselves Nebraskans. Like his father, Henry Fonda, who often lovingly expressed his fondness for our state and called it home, I believe Peter carries a special place in his heart, not only for Omaha, but also for Nebraska.

In 1959, when he played Elwood P. Dowd in *Harvey* at the Omaha Community Playhouse, Peter recalls:

"I was 19 and probably looked 12. My father came as a surprise without letting me know. He watched the performance and left. I got news later from his sister, my Aunt Harriet, that he really appreciated the performance. He said when young people try to play an older person, they go overboard with the shakes and dropsy, and I just went for the jokes—right for the laughs. That was nice to hear from him. It was quite a compliment.

"When I got home that night, I went to my room and thought very carefully, 'I'm able to make people believe I am a 72-year-old man with an 8-foot rabbit as a friend, which nobody can see. And I'm able to make people think I'm drunk on stage and I'm not.' I like this!

"If I don't have my own identity and I didn't then, by golly when I was out there on stage as Elwood P. Dowd, I knew my identity. I *was* Elwood P. Dowd. It made me feel comfortable and it made me feel accepted. It was then that my whole life changed in the beginning of 1959 in Omaha, Nebraska."

It was at that time that Peter wrote the letter to the Public Pulse of the *Omaha World-Herald*.

GREAT PLAINS FILM FESTIVAL

There had been discussion with Peter about the possibility of a Henry Fonda Film Festival in Grand Island. When we considered this at the Fonda ranch in Montana, Peter thought that Grand Island was a pretty uninviting place for a film festival. But, what we didn't know was that, only an hour or so away, the Great Plains Film Festival was happening in Lincoln, Nebraska. In July of 1997, Peter came to Lincoln to receive the Mary Riepma Ross Award for his significant impact on filmmaking as a product of the Great Plains.

My invitation read:

The Nebraska Film Office
Cordially invites you to attend
A reception for Peter and Becky Fonda
On July 24, 1997
At the home of
Christian Petersen
1315 S. 21st Street
Lincoln, Nebraska

GREAT PLAINS FILM FESTIVAL

And another:
> *In celebration of the Great Plains Film Festival*
> *in honor of Peter Fonda,*
> *you are invited to a cocktail buffet,*
> *5 to 7 p.m.*
> *at the home of Roger and Carol Sack*
> *followed by a screening of* Ulee's Gold.

Becky and I were on the phones making plans. We'd both be staying at the Cornhusker Hotel. As a friend of Peter and Becky's, I was sent an invitation to the reception, for which I thank Sandi Yoder and the Stuhr Museum. Going to this special event made it very special for me, for at last I could introduce the Fondas to my new Mr. Wonderful. The Fonda's had grieved with me after the loss of my dear Bob, and now they were to meet the new love of my life.

I had never attended a film festival before. It was great fun—the people, the stars, the writers, directors, producers, the parties, and the films that were shown. And the temperature outside was even on a high. We watched it climb to 101, 102, 103 degrees on the bank thermometer across the street from our hotel room. Peter seemed to love every minute, as the object of attention, and Becky was always concerned that he was OK.

It was an emotion-filled moment for Peter as he accepted the award. In his acceptance speech, he told of the good times he'd spent in Nebraska, and ended by saying, "I wish my Dad could be here to see this." Tears filled my eyes as he spoke of living with his beloved Aunt Harriet and attending school, and his times at the Omaha Community Playhouse. I couldn't help but think back to the letter he wrote; "I love Omaha."

THIS PLACE IN ALL ITS SEASONS

Peter Fonda and the author at the Great Plains Film Festival, Mary Riepma Ross Film Theater, Lincoln, Nebraska. (Ken Bolton)

BREAKFAST—TUPELO HONEY

During the event, we snatched little times together, but Becky had arranged that we have early Saturday morning breakfast in the hotel dining room. Other friends were to join us later and we would all go to the Farmers Market down in the Haymarket District of Lincoln. After "Good Mornings" and hugs all around and ordering our breakfast, I gave them my gift—a hand-carved folk art whirly-gig of an Indian with bow and arrow riding a racing horse.

And then Becky sat in front of me a quart jar wrapped in a green and yellow linen tea towel with the label: Grade A Tupelo Honey, gathered by Peter Fonda, 1996.

I cried. What a masterpiece!

MY FRIEND BECKY

"It is my friends that have made the story of my life."
—Helen Keller

*I*n the years since 1984, which I consider the beginning of the Fonda years of my life, much has been made possible by my friend Becky.

*"We cannot tell the precise moment when a friendship starts.
It is like filling a vessel drop...
by drop, which makes it at last run over;
so in a series of kindnesses there is at last one
which makes the heart run over."*
—James Boswell

Our friendship started, developed, and has continued to grow over the telephone lines that connect our two homes. This little chapter is dedicated to Davey Crockett's great-great-great-granddaughter, Henry Fonda's daughter-in-law, Jane Fonda's sister-in-law, wife to her "darling" Peter, stepmother to Bridgett and Justin, mother of Thomas, and grandmother to Thomas McGuane V. Her world is surrounded by family, a vastness of interesting and creative

MY FRIEND BECKY

friends of all walks of life, and her loving husband. She is a rancher, homemaker, reader of the *Farmer's Almanac*, lover of gardening, and a fabulous cook. Her kitchen is lined with First Place ribbons she has won at the County Fair. She makes her own catsup from her grandmother's recipe and spends hours making and canning apple butter and apple sauce from apples grown in their own apple orchard.

One late April morning, we talked. They had had two feet of snow on the ground during that night and it was still coming down. It was raining and lilac time in Nebraska. I gathered a bouquet of lilacs from my back yard and overnighted them to Becky. The next week, Becky sent me a picture of those lilacs in an antique vase gracing her living room coffee table. We do things like that.

She's bubbly. Her laugh is infectious. Her voice is like a melody. She is caring and funny, wears blue jeans and cowboy boots. She is petite and incredibly beautiful. "Bundle" is on her license plate. She loves the Fourth of July and savors their small town's old-fashioned holiday. She likes to shop in antique stores, boutique shops, and discount stores, where they save things for her. If you are lucky to be with her, you will meet everyone in Livingston, Montana, because she knows everyone and they know her. You will probably have lunch at Russell Chatham's Bar and Grille.

Her home is a log cabin with two great blue spruce trees in the front yard and a spectacular view. She may answer the phone while out walking the dogs. She appreciates nature and the simple things. She is a Crockett and a Fonda and as American as apple pie. Becky Fonda is a gift and I feel blessed to count her as one of my best friends.

> "To know someone here or there
> with whom you feel there is an understanding
> in spite of distances though unexpressed—
> that can make this earth a garden."
> —Goethe

SUE FONDA REMEMBERS...

During the Fonda years of my life, the Fonda family has shared many memories of Hank at different times and in different ways. So on this May 17, 1998, what would have been Henry Jaynes Fonda's 93rd birthday, the 2 P.M. program centered around the planting of several roses in his garden in the memory of two cousins, Douw and Henry. Sue Fonda of Denver, Douw's widow, wrote facts and memories of Hank and Douw to be read at the program.

A Cousin's Memories of Henry and Douw Fonda

About Henry

Since I knew him, Henry was always into some artistic project, or creative, anyway. When he came to Denver we were never sure what it would be. One time it was making terrariums. He went out and bought interesting glass bottles, many plants, and soil at the garden shop. Then wire, corks, and other hardware items to assemble and care for the project.

SUE FONDA REMEMBERS...

Another Christmas time it was macramé. He made hanging plant holders and belts of various kinds. When we were in Aspen for the holiday, Henry was not with the group, when asked where he was, his wife Shirlee replied, "Oh he's tied to some doorknob. He hasn't been loose since we arrived." True.

Then, there was the compost pile! He and Douw competed to see whose had the hottest internal temperature, the darkest soil, and the finest soil. Henry would even call from California to compare the inner temperature of the two piles. His always won. His perfection showed Douw up.

At Christmas and Thanksgiving, Henry was always in charge of the turkey, and he really reigned making "the day after turkey soup." That was a daylong affair and serious business with delicious results.

We've visited him on the outdoor sets when he's made movies. There is *a lot* of "down time." One time he was deeply into needlepoint. He made, at various times, beautiful chair covers for his dining room chairs, pillows, and a rug. Beautiful!! Designed perfectly. Some of his paintings were done between takes.

One time he started "project apple." We made apple pie, applesauce, apple Betty, and apple jelly. He flew to New York City with boxes of apples, and spent the next week learning how to make jelly and putting it up in quart jars!

That launched a series of apple paintings, really great ones. He then added his own orchard of miniature apple trees to his beautiful yard (trees brought in from the Northwest) in California. He already had an extensive vegetable garden and flower gardens fed by his compost pile. And he had chickens to furnish the fertilizer. One day, a huge swarm of bees descended on his yard. The "bee man" who came to the rescue put such enthusiasm into the event, Henry ended up becoming a beekeeper himself. He filled new paint cans with the wonderful honey, labeled them "Fonda Honey," and gave them as gifts. We still have one left.

Douw and Henry shared one deep passion; licorice. They kind of relished finding different, unusual containers for their caches and they sent each other supplies of the candy for various celebrations.

About Douw Fonda

Douw Fonda was born in Omaha September 30, 1912. As an adult, he did daytime soap operas on radio while studying drama. He was in a musical comedy, *Knickerbocker Holiday*, starring Walter Houston, directed by Josh Logan, for a long run on Broadway. He also acted in several Omaha Community Playhouse productions.

During World War II, he was an "expediter" for the Martin bomber plant in Omaha, securing priority materials from manufacturers throughout the East Coast. In 1947, after the war, Douw started his own manufacturers representative business in Denver covering the middle Rocky Mountain states, including Nebraska.

In 1949, he married Susan Ann Broadhurs in Denver. They had three daughters and six grandchildren. His interest included family, horses, and outdoor activities including jeeping, skiing, hiking, and picnics.

Douw was six and a half years younger than Henry but they were "pals" from childhood to his death. Douw and Henry shared many laughs and funny experiences—but my memory has lost many of them. Henry always could make Douw laugh with only a word or two, or a facial expression. So they had a good time together... Henry was Cyndi's godfather (my middle girl in Montana) and had to give Tina (girl #1) away at her wedding in Steamboat Springs in Colorado, as Douw had a relapse following an operation and Hank took over at the last minute.

Douw was the one who was the "lookout" when Henry and his pals smoked tobacco (or maybe it was corn silk) in the barn.

He acted as chauffeur when Henry took out a new girl he was trying to impress, even though he could hardly touch the pedals of the fancy borrowed car, and the visor of the hat Hank had gotten for him slipped down over his nose.

They put on plays and circuses directed by Hank and fully costumed on the raised driveway at Douw's house. Henry was usually the director.

Douw was always in awe when Henry would sit with a hunk of clay in his hands and mold Douw's face and expressions as he played a card game or assembled a puzzle.

Henry's family and Douw's spent almost every Sunday together; picnics were big on the summer agenda, and Douw's father was the official photographer. Almost all photos of the two families were taken by Ten Eyck Hilton Fonda and developed by him.

Harriet Fonda Warren, 1907-1998

Harriet Warren shared many family stories and information with me. Whenever she would write me a note, she ended with "give my friends at the Stuhr Museum my best." Much of the information in this book was from Harriet. She was pleased that I was writing it and I am sorry she will not be around to read it. She died July 16, 1998. Becky Fonda called me when Harriet died. Peter had talked to her on the phone just the day before. She was a beautiful lady and was loved by so many. The Omaha Community Playhouse lost a good friend. Special white roses (her favorite) were planted in the Henry Fonda Rose Garden in May of 1999 when we celebrated her brother's birthday. She was a member of our Friends of Henry Fonda group.

THIS PLACE IN ALL ITS SEASONS

She often mentioned her garden in her correspondence and, on my only visit to her home, she had just come into the house from the garden, complaining we needed a rain.

THE TURNER SANDHILLS RANCH

*I*n an *Omaha World-Herald* article, Ted Turner said he came to Nebraska because his wife Jane Fonda's family was from the state. "The Sandhills are very, very interesting," Turner said. "There is no other place on earth quite like them. It's really great. Everybody waves at everybody when you pass them in a car. It's fun to be in a place where there's a shortage of people, rather than an excess of them."

Once in a while, Turner is known to be waved over by a state patrolman for going too fast on those lonely open roads in our Sandhills country. He often has to show his driver's license, which reads Robert Edward Turner III, 1 CNN Center, Atlanta, Georgia.

Turner has become the nation's largest private landowner, along with owning the nation's largest private herd of bison—a once-threatened national symbol. Besides his ranch in Nebraska, he owns ranches with buffalo on them in New Mexico, Montana, and South Dakota.

FRIENDS OF HENRY FONDA

*F*onda Day in 1994 was the catalyst for forming the Friends of Henry Fonda. We are a group dedicated to preserving the works and promoting the life of Henry Fonda. The Friends is a non profit organization. There are four membership categories:
    Single...$15
    Mr. and Mrs...$20
    Emmy...$25
    Tony...$50
    Golden Globe...$100
    Oscar...$1,000

Jimmy Stewart and Dorothy McGuire are among the charter members. As a group, we have accomplished many things. An apple tree was planted in the backyard of Henry's home because he liked to raise apples. We planted and maintain a sundial rose garden and other gardens in the front yard.

On his birthday, we serve cake, fly kites, and give a scholarship each year to a Grand Island, Nebraska, drama student, and we sponsor a statewide contest for seventh through ninth grade art students. The four winners each receive $100 savings bond.

Our group is open to everyone and meets seven times a year in March, April, May, August, September, and November. In the months we don't have meetings, we care for the gardens, celebrate his birthday in May, make and serve apple cobbler at the annual Autumn Festival at the museum in September, and in December, decorate the Fonda cottage and host an annual Old-Fashioned Christmas. We worked with the United States Post Office to have an official Fonda Birth Home postmark, which was accomplished in 1994, and we are now are pursuing a postage stamp.

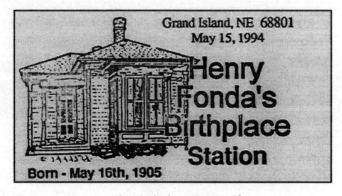

Fonda Birthplace Postmark

Friends of Henry Fonda work in Fonda cottage garden.

Fall decorations in the Fonda cottage garden

AFTERWARD
From the Grand Island Independent
(August, 1992)

Editorially speaking, Fonda represented the best of Nebraska. If there was a perfect image to represent the rugged and simple life of Central Nebraskans, it would be the bemusement once projected in the clear blue eyes of Henry Fonda. The rough but handsome features of his face seemed almost chiseled and hardened, but the smile and eyes were always kind. To even a stranger, Fonda projected himself as a rugged individual with a gentle nature. He looked the way that strong and independent men from the rural parts of our country ought to look. His direct and simplistic approach to life represents the demeanor most Nebraskans take. This Saturday, Stuhr Museum will present "A Tribute to Henry Fonda." An exhibit at Stuhr Museum's main gallery will cover several facets of the late actor's personal and professional life. The home in which he was born is now a part of the grounds' living history.

In 1978, an aging Fonda returned to Grand Island to see the home in which he was born, four years before his death in 1982. His visit was a brief one, but his ties to his background were strong. During a film in which Fonda read an essay about the state of Nebraska on Nebraska Educational Television, an emotional actor found himself describing Nebraska as home. In his ascent to acting greatness, Fonda relied on the qualities so abundant in his state. With the passage of time, a simplicity of life and total honesty became the lines written across his face.

In addition to Fonda, several notable actors, actresses, and personalities have transcended into the hearts of Americans through the media of filmmaking and television—Robert Taylor, David Jansen, Johnny Carson, Dick Cavett, and Sandy Dennis, to name just a few. In each case, these performers have projected a genuineness derived from childhood values that stress right from wrong and the importance of being a good friend and neighbor. In that sense, Fonda never really left Nebraska. He frequently referred to himself as "a Nebraska boy." The phrase seems to summarize his inherent kindness and humility. Beyond his acting greatness, Fonda created a special place in the hearts of his fellow Nebraskans. The fondness was as natural as it was reciprocal. He always carried Nebraska in his own heart.

THE FILMS OF HENRY FONDA

The Farmer Takes a Wife (1935)
Way Down East (1935)
I Dream Too Much (1935)
The Trail of the Lonesome Pine (1936)
The Moon's Our Home (1936)
Spendthrift (1936)
Wings of the Morning (1937)
You Only Live Once (1937)
Slim (1937)
That Certain Woman (1937)
I Met My Love Again (1938)
Jezebel (1938)
Blockade (1938)
Spawn of the North (1938)
The Mad Miss Manton (1938)
Jesse James (1939)
Let Us Live (1939)
The Story of Alexander Graham Bell
    (*The Modern Miracle in Great Britain*) (1939)
Young Mr. Lincoln (1939)
Drums Along the Mohawk (1939)

THIS PLACE IN ALL ITS SEASONS

The Grapes of Wrath (1940)
Lillian Russell (1940)
The Return of Frank James (1940)
Chad Hanna (1940)
The Lady Eve (1941)
The Immortal Sergeant (1943)
The Ox-Bow Incident (1943)
My Darling Clementine (1946)
The Long Night (1947)
The Fugitive (1947)
Daisy Kenyon (1947)
On Our Merry Way
    (released in Britain as *A Miracle Can Happen*) (1948)
Wild Geese Calling (1941)
You Belong to Me (1941)
The Male Animal (1942)
Rings On Her Fingers (1942)
The Magnificent Dope (1942)
Tales of Manhattan (1942)
The Big Street (1942)
Fort Apache (1948)
Jigsaw (1949)
Mister Roberts (1955)
War and Peace (1956)
The Wrong Man (1956)
The Tin Star (1957)
12 Angry Men (1957)
Stage Struck (1958)
Warlock (1959)
The Man Who Understood Women (1959)
Advise and Consent (1962)
The Longest Day (1962)
How the West Was Won (1963)
Spencer's Mountain (1963)

THE FILMS OF HENRY FONDA

The Best Man (1964)
Fail Safe (1964)
Sex and the Single Girl (1964)
The Rounders (1965)
In Harm's Way (1965)
Battle of the Bulge (1965)
A Big Hand for the Little Lady (1966)
The Dirty Game (1966)
Welcome to Hard Times (1967)
Firecreek (1968)
Yours, Mine and Ours (1968)
Madigan (1968)
The Boston Strangler (1968)
One Upon a Time in the West (1969)
Too Late the Hero (1970)
There Was a Crooked Man (1970)
The Cheyenne Social Club (1970)
Sometimes a Great Notion (1971)
The Serpent (1972)
My Name is Nobody (1973)
Ash Wednesday (1973)
Midway (1976)
Rollercoaster (1977)
Tentacles (1977)
The Great Smokey Roadblock (also *The Last of the Cowboys*) (1977)
The Swarm (1978)
Fedora (1978)
Meteor (1979)
City on Fire (1979)
Wanda Nevada (1979)
Battle of Mareth (also known as *The Greatest Battle*) (1979)
On Golden Pond (1981)

BOOKLIST

Fonda—My Life by Howard Teichman
The Fondas by John Springer
The Films and Careers of Henry, Jane, and Peter Fonda Citadel Press
Henry Fonda by Norm Goldstein and the Associated Press
Henry Fonda, A Biography by Allan Roberts
The Fondas—A Hollywood Dynasty
Excerpts from magazines and newspapers

ABOUT THE AUTHOR

Ruth McCauley is a Nebraskan proud of her ties to Grand Island, Nebraska which has been her home since 1955. She has been the spearhead in creating the Friends of Henry Fonda. She is involved in the planning and promotion of most of the activities at the Henry Fonda cottage on the grounds of the Stuhr Museum of the Prairie Pioneer.

After raising a family, Ruth began a successful business and design career with sales of her products going to Bloomingdales in New York City and accounts in Paris. Upon her retirement, she began writing *This Place in all Its Seasons: The Henry Fonda Home in Nebraska*.

She continues to decorate for Christmas and help with the birthday party for Henry in May.